INTRODUCTION

The UNIVERSAL TRAVELER is more than a guide to creative problem-solving and clear thinking; it is your passport to success. The process described is universally relevant; based on the premise that any problem, dream, or aspiration, no matter its size or degree of complexity, can benefit from the same logical and orderly 'systematic' process employed to solve world-level problems. Only the wording and methods vary and then, in appearance alone. Systematic process, derived from the study of human control systems known as Cybernetics, forms the basis for modeling most social, industrial, and economic problem situations. To provide an everyday application of method leading to a more orderly life process, we have translated the technical terminology of systematic problem-solving into conversational language and simplified techniques. The resulting 'user-friendly' approach to problem-solving is called SOFT SYSTEMS. Once learned and internalized with practice, the Universal Traveler "soft systematic" approach will allow anyone to deal more logically and orderly with all manner of problem situations or goals.

Library of Congress Cataloging-in-Publication Data
Koberg, Don, 1930-
The universal traveler : a soft-systems guide to
creativity,problem-solving, and the process of reach-
ing goals / by Don Koberg and Jim Bagnall.-- 4th ed.
    p. cm.
    Includes bibliographical references and index.
    ISBN 1-56052-679-3 (pbk.)
    1. Problem solving. 2. Creative ability. 3. Goal
(Psychology)
    I. Bagnall, Jim. II. Title.
    BF441.K55 2003
    158.1--dc21
    2003007910

Previous editions through 2003 number at least 16
printings
03 04 05 06 10 9 8 7 6 5 4 3 2 1
Printed in the United States of America

the ANATOMY of the Universal Traveler

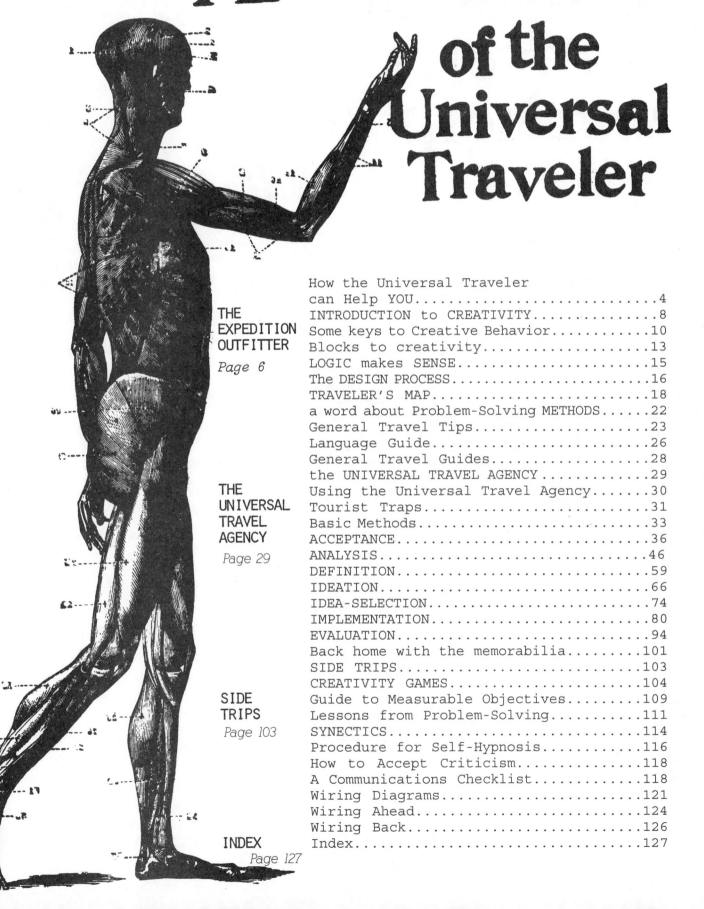

THE
EXPEDITION
OUTFITTER

Page 6

THE
UNIVERSAL
TRAVEL
AGENCY

Page 29

SIDE
TRIPS

Page 103

INDEX

Page 127

How the Universal Traveler can help YOU

Using the analogy of travel, an activity already known to all readers, The UNIVERSAL TRAVELER makes the process of problem-solving a familiar activity. The travel vocabulary reinforces the concept that design is more meaningful when it can be visualized and pursued as a logical and planned journey through a series of stopovers called DESIGN STAGES. Although chance and random process are not excluded, their application depends on how appropriate they may be in specific situations.

Before setting out on any journey, it is well to visit THE EXPEDITION OUTFITTER. There you will find general information, tools, and additional references in the form of TRAVEL TIPS, LANGUAGE GUIDES, including an all-important TRAVELER'S MAP.

The heart of this book, The TRAVEL AGENCY, contains advice for journeys of all kinds. In it you will find methods for getting started and proceeding along various stops on your itinerary to reach a planned destination. A variety of alternative travel methods is offered, emphasizing the choice of movement or transition from one leg (stage) to another within the total sequence of steps in the journey (process). Sub-divided into the seven major 'design stages' of the 'design process', The TRAVEL AGENCY allows travelers to experience the process in a personalized and efficient manner.

The final section of the book contains SIDE TRIPS with suggestions for additional possibilities for enhancing or enriching any journey to make it more enjoyable and meaningful.

Since all travel guides are forever in need of updating, so THE UNIVERSAL TRAVELER has been printed with a wide margin on each page to provide plenty of room for personal travel notes. As you discover ideas and invent methods of your own, pencil them in on their appropriate pages. It is but another 'method' that can save having to rediscover them on subsequent trips.

You bought it; make it yours. Often wellworn, stained and dog-eared, those books most treasured are generally the ones most used. Since The Universal Traveler has been designed to serve as a companion for the typical problem-solving voyager, you can make it your own and thereby increase its personal value by adding notes, sketches, inserts, underscores, paste-ins, writeovers, and yes, even scratch-outs.

BON VOYAGE

Get everything you need to take along at

the
EXPEDITION
OUTFITTER

✓ *hiking boots*
rain slicker
fur-lined gloves
✓ *safety matches*
hat
flashlight
✓ *batteries*

The EXPEDITION OUTFITTER stocks the basic
requirements for a more satisfying problem-
solving journey. You will find a "map" out-
lining a typical problem-solving expedition
as well as notes on CREATIVITY and its destructive counterpart FEAR. Also available
are METHODS, TIPS, TOURIST TRAPS and a list
of GUIDES other travelers have followed to
successful solutions and goal achievement.

 BE PREPARED! Sufficient supplies and equip-
ment can improve the odds for success of any
voyage. When your gear is incomplete or mis-
matched to the situation everything else
seems to lose importance. Basic requirements
must be given top priority. When planning a
hike into the wilderness, compass, map,
matches, hat and sturdy boots come first;
frills and extras can be added later if
space and time allow.

After visiting The EXPEDITION OUTFITTER, you
may find it helpful to breeze through the
entire book. Familiarity with its overall
contents will put you in a better position
to customize the material to your liking as
it is encountered. For example, near the end
of the book in SIDE TRIPS, the Guide to Measurable Objectives can save time and energy
along the way and might be put to immediate
use at the outset of your trip.

However excited to get going you may be,
take it slowly and easily the first few
times through the process. Travel is much
more meaningful and definitely more fun when
not rushed.

INTRODUCTION to CREATIVITY

Life is a continual sequence of encounters. Some are unavoidable; to be enjoyed or suffered by choice. Others can be controlled consciously. Creative problem-solving is a process of dealing intelligently with those situations that can be controlled. A creative problem-solver is a 'designer'; a person intending to improve what exists or to find clear paths through dilemmas or challenging situations and arrive at satisfying solutions.

In general, in order to improve something and do it creatively, it is necessary, first, to identify what it is that actually needs improving; second, to understand the interactive factors involved; and third, to develop the required skills and tools (methods) to manage the task.

Creative Behavior differs from normal behavior which is either primarily objective or primarily subjective. Creativity requires a willingness to join subjectivity with objectivity. It involves learning to think and behave "wholly" instead of one way or another; to alternate between what you sense or feel, what you already know or think you know, and what you might discover by trying something new. The primarily OBJECTIVE person, for example, knows everything by name. Once named, no further examination of content is required thereby eliminating the potential for deeper understanding and ionovation. The primarily SUBJECTIVE person, being a here-and-now sense-response mechanism, continually delights in sensory experience and cares little for names or other fixed conclusions.

TO COMBINE THE TWO, thus creating a more natural balance between the extremes of sensing and knowing, IS TO GAIN MORE THAN BOTH. The combination allows you to deal more completely with any encounter.

Creative wholeness leads beyond the here and now of sensory response and remembered experience and knowledge. It opens the gate to a deeper understanding of the natural balance between divergent and convergent thinking and the freedom to control your behavior.

Allowing yourself to alternate between thinking and feeling may be difficult at first. Adults live in social virtual worlds of words and symbols. It is only human to become more objective and less subjective with age. Knowing the names of things saves you lots of time and stopping to smell the roses or enjoy reality is considered a waste of time. It may require frequent practice to overcome the habits related to 'normal' behavior. It is far more 'normal' to "think" all day long and save "feeling" for "after work" or the weekend. Because of being unique, balanced behavior is often viewed as careless or maladjusted and even at times subversive to the institutions that normalcy creates to perpetuate normalcy. Since conformity is the shortest route to acceptance in a mass society, behaving uniquely is a sure way to become an outcast. But acceptable unique behavior is possible for anyone, who by intention is adventurous, pride-less, self-disciplined and self-believing, who has interest in resolving problematic conditions, and who continually develops an ability to be "whole." When learned, the new behavior will seem every bit as natural as the old.

In brief, CREATIVITY doesn't come free. It is not a gift or quirk of birth. Some people don't "just have it" while others do not. Nor does it come from luck or magic. Creativity is learnable behavior requiring steady and determined effort. If you accept the fact that the goal of creativity is innovation, you should realize that creating something "new" is NOT NORMAL but DIFFERENT from normal, perhaps even 'abnormal.'

CAUTION!! If you believe you are behaving creatively and your behavior is readily accepted in normal society, one of two conditions is probable: either you have conditioned society to accept your abnormal actions or your input is really not as unique as it seems.

Some keys to Creative Behavior

Practiced creative behavior breeds automatic creative behavior. Said another way, creativity and consciousness of procedures (process) and methods go hand in hand. If you become more aware of your position relative to what has gone before and what is yet to come, your ability to decide from both the broad view and the specific view is increased allowing you to become more accurate in your predictions and choices throughout every journey.

Proven suggestions for developing consciousness of creative procedure and methodology are:

1. FREEDOM FROM PRIDE (SELF-DISCIPLINE)
2. BELIEF IN SELF AND THE ABILITY TO SUCCEED
3. CONSTRUCTIVE DISCONTENT
4. WHOLENESS
5. ABILITY TO CONTROL HABIT

FREEDOM FROM PRIDE (SELF-DISCIPLINE)

1

Pride, other than as respect for quality or achievement, is destructive counter-creative behavior and detracts from the attainment of goals. It is difficult to see clearly with your nose in the air. PRIDE stands in the way of creativity by inhibiting you from asking key questions, thus stifling the key requisite for curiosity. It restricts a change of mind or direction which thereby fixes a preconceived and prejudicial course. And it runs counter to the true selflessness required for the "giving" of oneself to the task! Pride joins the other "deadly sins" to detract from improvement. SELF-DISCIPLINE, i.e., "being true to your self", on the other hand, is a truth-revealing behavior. It requires courage of conviction and fearless acceptance of the responsibility for being what you are, and taking steps to insure improvement. Modifying behavior to meet specific situations need not limit freedom or work against the needs of others involved.

2 BELIEF IN SELF AND THE ABILITY TO SUCCEED

Be self-motivated! Belief in your ability to succeed is necessary for both motivation and the maintenance of creative inertia. If you wait for someone else to move you, you might find yourself headed in a wrong direction.

Ego-strength and leadership are closely related. Leaders with low self-belief are rare. The norm is to subdue ego and become a follower; to play the social game of self-denial and make less of your abilities and potentials. Hiding your ego from others results in denying it to yourself. The deeper you bury it, the less it serves you as part of your behavior. Begin to believe in your own creative potential and you will begin to behave more creatively."

3 CONSTRUCTIVE DISCONTENT

Discontent is as prerequisite to meaningful problem-solving as is dissent to being a good citizen. Adolescence is usually all that is required for achieving half of this important attribute of creativity. A "contented" teen is rare indeed; discontent goes with that time of life. To the young, everything needs improvement. Yet, it is usually the lack of a constructive attitude that wins out in the end, turning potentially healthy "discontent" into nothing more than moans and groans.

Constructive discontent is a necessity for the creative problem-solver. With maturity, your discontent wanes. Society teaches that "fault-finders" disturb the status quo. It soon seems "good" not to "make waves" or "rock the boat" and "let sleeping dogs lie" and "be seen but not heard." Only a constructive attitude can maintain the once dynamic condition.

WHOLENESS

Everyone both senses and knows. It is natural to both feel and to think or decide.
With age the more you know, the less you
tend to feel. It's faster that way. A normal
adult will smother sensitivity in favor of
automatic judgment and moving on to new
knowledge. But remaining sensitive doesn't
mean re-learning the same things over and
over again. It simply allows for a more
balanced whole. By alternating between feeling and knowing, between sensing and deciding in a conscious way, you maintain control
of your **WHOLE** potential.

ABILITY TO CONTROL HABIT

Behavior in general is a combination of
habits. Habits simplify life. They develop
from discoveries turned to beliefs and actions which, when repeated until memorized,
become automatic. Since the majority of
basic discoveries occur during childhood,
most habits and resultant behaviors form
early and strengthen with age. As habits
work for you, they can also work against
you. The habit of believing you know something so well that it preempts discovery
always works against you in terms of behaving creatively.

In order to see things differently and become more innovative, it is necessary to be
in control of habits...always ready to take
an unknown path and to chance the unproven
by developing new, replacement habits when
the old ones get in the way. In the end,
only your value judgment determines how
helpful or hindering your habits are in
terms of personal problem-solving ability.

Blocks to creativity

It is normal to hold back because of being wary of making mistakes or asking 'dumb' questions. Yet few errors carry stiff penalties and the asking of any question, no matter how innocent, suggests willingness to learn. The most common barriers to creative behavior are self-generated pride, fear, jealousy and competitiveness. The creatively active person is not put off by such demons.

fear

The thought of having a truly new idea can be scary. By definition, the inventor (creator of new ideas) is automatically a minority of one.

FEAR of making mistakes
FEAR of being seen as a fool
FEAR of being exposed as ignorant
FEAR of being criticized for failure
FEAR of offending others
FEAR of being "alone"
FEAR of making waves
FEAR of being associated with taboos
FEAR of losing the security of habit
FEAR of losing the love of the group
FEAR of taking a stand and having to defend
   it
FEAR of being unable to take the heat

fear

Fear stems from lack of preparation and the
accompanying anxiety when dealing with the
unknown.

Since creative problem-solving suggests diving head-first into the unknown, fear might
be your most formidable enemy. Being afraid
is both natural and normal. Trying to be
fearless is risky business since fear evokes
caution which at times can be a life-saver.
But when caution deters progress and creativity through misdirecting your energy,
it is working against you.

It's unreasonable to imagine escaping fear
altogether. But by changing your focus from
"I'm afraid to be wrong" to "I'm trying to
be right," the positive point of view can
help in overcoming this major block to a
more creative life.

Humans are social creatures and no healthy
person would enjoy being an outcast. But
behaving 'off the wall' or 'out of the box'
can make you just that. Fear of being alone,
apart from the norm, stops most people from
even considering doing or saying something
that might be judged as unusual.

Then again, what if you do try something
unusual which turns out to be all wrong?
Will you be judged as a fool? The mere
thought of wearing a dunce cap is enough to
stop normal people in their tracks. It is
true that the plane could crash and the boat
could sink but the odds against either disaster happening keep air and sea lanes
busy. Only self-belief, the hope of being
right instead of wrong, can outweigh such
fears.

In essence logic helps us to understand how all things are or can be organized and inter-related. It is a basis or foundation on which to build. It is an ordering system within which we can deal with pieces and not lose sight of the totality that contains them. Logic is a way, an orderly way, to include sensory response in a conscious process.

IN SHORT...

LOGIC
makes
SENSE

(Organized knowing develops meaningful feeling.)

LOGIC is both basis and context for order.
LOGIC is a guide for mental activity.
LOGIC is devoid of everyday linguistic
    content...It has no semantics.
LOGIC is syntax rather than definition.
LOGIC is a structure for reason.
LOGIC is a series of operations or methodi-
    cal transformations.
LOGIC is neither metaphysical nor philo-
    sophical.
LOGIC is the basis of scientific
    methodology.
LOGIC provides an organizational framework.
LOGIC is in flux.
LOGIC simplifies process.

The DESIGN PROCESS is a Problem-Solving JOURNEY

Gym teachers and geologists, writers and truck farmers, movie makers and motorcyclists, audiophiles and elevator operators, xylophonists and sci-fi fans are all problem-solvers. Everyone is a problem-solver. Some just do it better than others, by design. By generating unique and/or particularly satisfying solutions, a designer is said to behave creatively. Since problem-solving is intertwined with living, you are ever embarking on a problem-solving journey of one sort or another. The more you understand DESIGN as being closely related to the life process the better you'll be as a creative problem-solver or 'designer'.

The creative problem-solving (design) process is most easily understood as a sequence of stages or stopovers on a journey to a given destination. A full round-trip itinerary offers experience at each of those places. Once internalized through experience, design process oriented travel involves the conscious application of incentives, intentions, decisions, actions and evaluations.

Note: The design process presented here is a design in itself; developed by extracting the essential characteristics of many specific problem-solving processes, including the works of Wallas, Dewey, Rossman, Guilford, Osborn, Stanislawski, Barnes, Gordon, Kepner-Tregoe, Arnold, Churchman, Zwicky, General Electric, the Military, and PERT (Program Evaluation Review Technique).

DESIGNER = LIFE LIVER = CREATIVE PROBLEM SOLVER

A COMPLETE SYSTEMATIC PROBLEM-SOLVING JOURNEY includes a SEVEN STAGE ITINERARY.

GETTING STARTED

Stating initial intentions; accept the problem as a challenge; allowing the problem to become the generator of process; self-motivation.

GATHERING FACTS AND FEELINGS

Becoming familiar with the insides and outsides of the problem; discovering what the "world of the problem" contains.

DETERMINING THE DESTINATION (ESSENTIALS FOR SUCCESS)

Determining the main issues of the problem; conceptualizing and clarifying aims, ends, and goals of problem resolution.

GENERATING ALTERNATIVES

Identifying all possible ways of realizing the goals.

CHOOSING FROM THE OPTIONS

Comparing the destination with the possible ways of getting there; determining the best match(es).

TAKING ACTION

Giving form to the selected "best ways;" "realizing" intentions.

MEASURING SUCCESS

Reviewing the journey to determine the degree of success and its overall value; what was learned? How can the experience be used to make future travel more meaningful and/or enjoyable?

Denver

WHAT'S BOSTON ALL ABOUT. What lies between here and there? What should I be looking for? Who do I know there? etc., etc.

Why do I want to go? What's so good about Boston anyway? What does Boston offer to me?

analyze

TRAVELER'S MAP

Phoenix

accept situation

Start Finish

evaluate

HEY, THAT WAS A GREAT TRIP.

San Francisco

Did we get to Boston like we planned? Did it make sense to go at all?

Did we encounter contingencies that changed our initial goals? How come San Francisco looks so different now?

INITIAL STATEMENT OF OBJECTIVE: "Lets go to Boston. I've always wanted to go there. Why? Because I'm an American History Freak.

define

WHAT DO I THINK THE PROBLEM
OF GOING TO BOSTON REALLY IS?

ANSWER: Having a happy trip, seeing at
least ten states, learning about U. S. history,
on $50.00

St. Louis

ideate

Cincinnati

*An excursion through the
Process of Design
is like taking a round-trip
from San Francisco to
Boston*

NOW THAT I KNOW WHAT I THINK THE
PROBLEM REALLY IS ... WHAT ARE
ALL THE WAYS I CAN GET IT ON.
ANSWER:
    I could: hitch a ride, stay with
    friends, walk, work along the
    way, ride my bike, get a job on
    the railroad, etc,etc.

Boston

New York

select

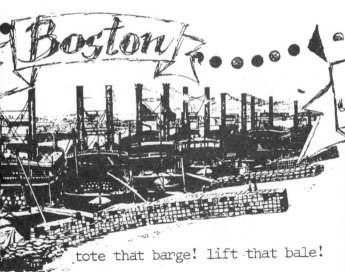

tote that barge! lift that bale!

COMPARING GOALS WITH IDEAS

Well that solves it. I'll hitch
to Phoenix, get a job for a week,
train to Denver and stay with ...
etc., etc.

implement

About ANALYSIS and SYNTHESIS

When comparing varied approaches to problem-solving it soon becomes clear that certain common-denominators exist which unite them all. In particular, two "basic" stages emerge. The first is ANALYSIS or breaking the whole into parts for closer examination. The second is SYNTHESIS or resolving the examined parts to form a new whole.

analysis ➔ synthesis

The need to apply what is learned from Analysis to form a Synthesis, a third connective link or bridge is often suggested. When included, the basic process becomes

analysis ➔ definition ➔ synthesis

Further sub-division becomes personal and specific or dependent on the type of problem considered. In general terms, Synthesis, for example, breaks down into idea-finding, idea-selecting and action-taking. If Acceptance is added at the beginning and Evaluation tacked onto the end, a sequence of seven activities evolves. That seven stage process is presented in the following pages.

accept situation ➔ analyze ➔ define ➔ ideate ➔ select ➔ implement ➔ evaluate

If orderly thinking seems as if it might hamper your creative freedom, try to realize that most procedures can be viewed or applied in a variety of ways. How you see something is largely up to you. Procedural stages need not follow one another linearly like coaches of a train where moving forward depends on passing through successive cars one at a time. There are other versions.

20

feedback

You might view the stages of process as a back and forth action where you never go forward without always looping back to check on yourself; where progress only occurs by looking backward before moving forward.

branching

You might go on and on, never stopping, solving one problem after another or dealing with the same problem again and again, and always getting a bit closer to perfection.

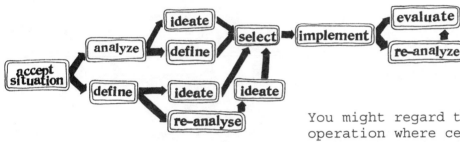

You might regard the design process as an operation where certain events occurring at various stages determine more than one connection and progress to a resolution is more expansive than direct.

● ● ●

circular

Of course the most natural way to view process is as a scattering of pieces with each stage progressing concurrently with the others rather than as a connected chain of events...more like a horse race—with each stage competing for attention—than like a mule-train - which is straight-forward and linear but more easily controlled.

In all cases, the important thing to realize is that although only one horse may be out front at any moment, the others are also part of the race and that each stage is always in process, i.e., the problem-solver is rarely relieved from dealing with all stages of accepting, analyzing, defining, ideating, deciding, acting, and evaluating throughout the process.

In reality the conscious solving of problems and the PROBLEM-SOLVING PROCESS does proceed endlessly. The ultimate version would have to be SPIRAL—a continuum of sequential round-trips progressing ad infinitum like entwined atoms within a DNA molecule.

a word about Problem-Solving Methods

Because travel usually entails trying the untried, it can at times be complex and frustrating. Learning 'how to' travel becomes a necessity. Much like selecting the route, side roads, and overnight stops for travel, choosing and tailoring methods to fit both problem and problem-solver is a separate task within each problem-solving journey.

Along with their other supplies, experienced travelers (creative problem-solvers) usually keep notes to remind them of the best ways to get from place to place. Such information regarding technique or approach is called 'method.'

DESIGN METHODS are practical ways for getting from one design stage to another. Creating your own design methods is easy once you realize they need not be complex or formal. You already have favorites, perhaps not consciously named or controlled, but ways that are particularly yours from previous use. Giving names to methods is an ideal method in itself. It is a way to improve remembering a particular technique. There are as many different methods as there are people with needs for methods. A universally common method of making notes, for example, is called by dozens of different names.

Observation suggests that complex problems may require complex techniques while simple problems might be handled more basically. Then again, in spite of logic, the reverse might also be valid. In any event, you should understand that just as you wouldn't choose a moving van to go get the groceries, you wouldn't choose computerized techniques in order to make a decision from a lunch menu...but you could if it became appropriate to a specific situation like selecting for thousands of delegates at a political convention.

the BEST technique is the ONE which works BEST for YOU!

General Travel Tips

Before setting out on a journey you may want to consider the following "tips" from seasoned travelers.

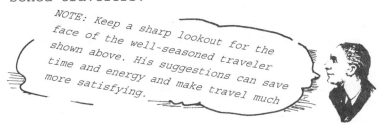

NOTE: Keep a sharp lookout for the face of the well-seasoned traveler shown above. His suggestions can save time and energy and make travel much more satisfying.

If you can't explain where you're headed, you'll never know when you've arrived.

To get what you want you've got to give up wanting and start working on the process of making it happen.

The creative person is both a problem-maker and a problem-solver. Satisfaction with status quo sends creativity packing.

Know your limits in order to stretch them painlessly. Take care to not become an "impossible dreamer."

Commencement has two meanings: to finish and to begin. The end of one journey merely marks the beginning of another.

Ideas are a "dime-a-dozen." It is only after being translated into physical form or practice that an idea becomes valuable.

A problem is merely another "situation in need of improvement."

To be whole, theory and practice must combine. "Talking about a problem" needs to be balanced by "dealing with it."

Attitudes change with practical experience. Learn by doing.

To learn, try teaching. No student ever learns as much as the teacher.

Inventions are easy to imagine. Giving them form and making them work is the hard part.

Relaxation during the process of problem-solving allows for "incubation." You need time to "digest" before chewing some more.

Defer Judgment until all the facts are known. False expectation can make the journey meaningless.

Habit-breaking is a creative necessity. Try not to get so locked into a habit that it will cost you heavily to break.

Methods are tools that make problem-solving easier. It makes sense to have a varied assortment available.

Don't select a path that feels wrong. But realize that even new shoes can seem strange until broken in.

Get friendly with your problems. Talk with them. Listen to their needs. Write about them. Take their "temperature."

 The anxiety of procrastination can be easily replaced by the joy of getting started.

 Caution: Using the same method over and over again may become hazardous to your problem-solving health. Pioneers know there are many ways to skin a cat.

 Rather than saving evaluation until the end, make incremental notes and improvements as you go.

 Knowledge is what you feel to be true from experience. The rest is conjecture or faith.

 The values of ideas change with time and use. What looks ripe today can become moldy tomorrow.

 The profession with the brightest future is that of creative problem-solving. The statute of limitations on problem-solutions is short.

 The process-oriented problem-solver is a good record-keeper. Meaningful evaluation relies on bits and pieces collected along the way.

 Dealing with general problems requires knowledge of generalized principles. As innovator Buckminster Fuller suggested, design requires "getting a really grand strategy for dealing with the whole."

Every problem situation is unique. Solutions require that specific dependent and independent variables be identified and understood.

Language Guide

OTHER WAYS OF SAYING THE SAME THING

Paraphrasing, i.e., using other words for describing a thought, object, or subject, is a self-teaching method. By asking for other or additional ways to describe a thing, a familiarity develops. A Language Guide appears within each section that follows. To get the ball rolling, here are some other ways to describe subjects we've already encountered.

A PROBLEM IS...
..."a situation in need of improvement" (Osborn-Parnes)
..."an excursion" (Gordon)
...an unfulfilled intention, plan, or desired outcome
...a disorganized group of pieces awaiting unification
...acknowledged difficulty
...a barrier or obstacle to the satisfaction of need
...a constructive purpose
...an unrealized dream
...an instability or imbalance; a disharmony; a disorder ...disunity

A SUCCESSFUL SOLUTION...
...enhances a defined purpose
...achieves the pre-stated end(s)
...satisfies a conscious intent
...frees the problem-solver for other activities
...helps to further clarify value and purpose

DESIGN PROCESS IS...
...a way to maximize goals
...a concept for optimizing objectives
...a technique for realizing intentions
...a scheme for giving form to intentions
...a sequence of operations leading to an end
...a means of anticipatory improvement
...a bridging of analysis to synthesis via concept
...a recipe for managing parts and pieces of a dilemma
...a plan for organizing and dealing with data
...a logical means to realize a dream

A DESIGN METHOD IS...

...a technique for moving from place to place
...a problem-solving tool
...a strategy or 'trick'
...a means or way of performing an operation
...a recipe or guide to achievement
...a mini-process or procedure

A CREATIVE PROBLEM-SOLVER IS...

...innovative and ever-renewing
...a dealer in options and decisions
...procedural and methodological
...a skilled habit-maker and habit-breaker
...a divergent-convergent thinker
...rhythmical, thoughtful and sensitive
...a fearless adventurer and a cautious planner
...both off-center and in-line
...non-normal; consciously different when necessary
...a thinking-feeling person
...a lovable jerk; one who subverts in an acceptable way
...accepting (open-minded, relaxed, brave, adaptable)
...analytic (curious, interested, fact-gatherer)
...definitive (conceptual, insightful, purposeful)
...idea-prone (free-wheeling, inventive)
...selective (decisive, assertive, discerning, assured)
...active (self-motivated, dedicated, constructive)
...evaluative (judgmental, objective, critical)
...an independent "both/and-either/or" person

REVIEW

Solving problems is a universal occupation. Small or large, personal or social, you are always busy trying to resolve one problem situation or another. What to do to pass a course? Which subject to choose for a project or term paper? What to do tonight? Which color to select? How to improve the back yard? Where to get the money for a trip abroad? Where to begin looking for a job? How to stop pollution? How to start? How to keep going? How to stop? What's the next step?

Problem situations rarely arrive pre-di-
gested and clearly presented for easy management. More than likely they will be
tangled within other situations, disguised
or innocent appearing and/or locked inside
some emotional distress or values conflict.
It's possible to spend all your time and
energy trying to untangle the pre-problem
mess before ever getting into the real meat
of the situation.

Although potential problems surround you in
many apparently different forms, it is only
their specific situations that differ. Aside
from dealing with external situations, some
problems originate inside your head. You
invent them. Some you easily recognize as
problems and proceed to solve them; some are
merely accepted as ongoing givens. They
might involve contrary goals, confused values, and hidden biases. Some problems seem
impossible to solve; others don't seem like
problems at all. In any case, the process of
solving or resolving them creatively by design is basically the same.

General Travel Guides

Altshuller, Genrich, Technology Innovation,
1999 THE INNOVATION ALGORITHM: TRIZ

Adams, James, Perseus Books, 2001
CONCEPTUAL BLOCKBUSTING

DeBono, Edward, Little Brown, 1999
SIX THINKING HATS

Checkland, Peter, Wiley, 1999
SYSTEMS THINKING, SYSTEMS PRACTICE

Jones, Morgan, Times Books, 1998
THE THINKER'S TOOLKIT

Jones, John Christopher, John Wiley & Sons,
1997 DESIGN METHODS

McKim, Robert, Pearson Learning, 1997
THINKING VISUALLY

Thorpe, Scott, Sourcebooks, Inc., 2001
HOW TO THINK LIKE EINSTEIN

NOTE: Up-to-date sources for persons and
links to organizations dealing with creativity can be found at
www.creativityforyou.com
and
www.creativityatwork.com

·the·
···UNIVERSAL···
TRAVEL AGENCY

A storehouse of means & methods for getting from
☞HERE☞ ☞THERE☞

Using the Universal Travel Agency

Planning a problem-solving trip? The Travel Agency offers help and advice on every aspect of getting from where you are to where you hope to be. It is here where you can discover many and various methods for wending your way through the problem-solving process and doing it in a creative way.

The seven sections within the "Agency" represent individual stages of a sequential problem-solving journey or design process.

Although sequential progress through the seven stages is theoretically more efficient, thus generally ideal for novice users, it is also possible to vary the sequence in accord with the specific demands of individual problems and problem-solvers. Be aware of jumping too far ahead. Information passed over or missed could lead to pitfalls. In the end, the most logical procedure is that special series of events that works best for you and your situation.

Tourist Traps

 **1** INTUITION CAN GET IN YOUR WAY
Trust and respect your intuition. It embodies your background knowledge and is your basic reference data-bank. Being insightful is to allow your past to serve as a guide to your future...but don't allow insight to control every decision. Fresh analysis can change everything you think.

 **2** TOOL UP IN ADVANCE. Don't be caught without your camera or other record-keeping device such as a notebook, sketchbook, recorder, etc. Good records often eliminate the need to re-discover experiences over and over before realizing their importance. Merely talking about an experience is a proven method for learning its benefits and shortcomings.

 **3** SLEEPING AT THE WHEEL
Don't wait until you're half-way there to realize you've been missing much of the action. Attempting to recreate experience without "sensory notes" can cause you to miss even more. KEEP ALL YOUR SENSES AWAKE and you'll increase the value and enjoyment of any process.

 **4** PUNY TRAVELERS MISS A LOT
Problem-solving travelers need to rely on both physical and mental health in order to function completely and properly. It's a cinch that when you don't feel well, whether consciously or subconsciously, you won't operate at full potential.

 **5** TRY TO STAY CALM by self-control. Too much coffee or tea will only shatter your nerves.

SNACK CAUTIOUSLY. A high-protein peanut butter sandwich can help you stay the course longer than a high-energy short-lasting candy bar.

 **6** DON'T EXPECT SUCCESS FROM WORK WITHOUT REST. When tired, take a break. Then proceed on your journey with renewed energy.
BEWARE OF OVERVALUING EARLY SUCCESS.

After the inertia is broken there is usually much more traveling to do. Similarly, if a "first" idea is not properly evaluated in terms of overall objectives and ends up being your "only" idea, it can cause even more trouble. Remaining conscious of the entire PROCESS at every stage allows you to consider new alternatives and to make your limitations and your objectives as you go.

DON'T BE FRIGHTENED BY BIGNESS. There are tools for dealing with all contexts, large or small. Seek the tools that fit the task. A consciously-applied PROCESS-METHOD combination can smooth out even the most unfriendly or unfamiliar appearing situation.

EXPERIENCE IS THE BEST TEACHER. Relax and learn. You will only be "at home" with what you discover to be true yourself.

DON'T BE HALF-WITTED. Knowledge acquired with age creates a tendency to cease exploration and to become a KNOW-IT-ALL or SENSE-IT-NOT. Remember that wholeness requires both sensitivity and knowledge. It helps to enhance curiosity, uniqueness, doing the unexpected and adventure. The older, more educated and experienced you become, the more you know and the less sense you imagine to need.

THINK BEFORE YOU LEAP. Quick solutions to unstudied and undefined problems can be even more problematic after the fact. When problem situations arise take some side trips to Analysis and Definition before jumping to answers and conclusions. Instead of asking "What can I do about some apparent problem" stop to question whether or not a true problem exists.

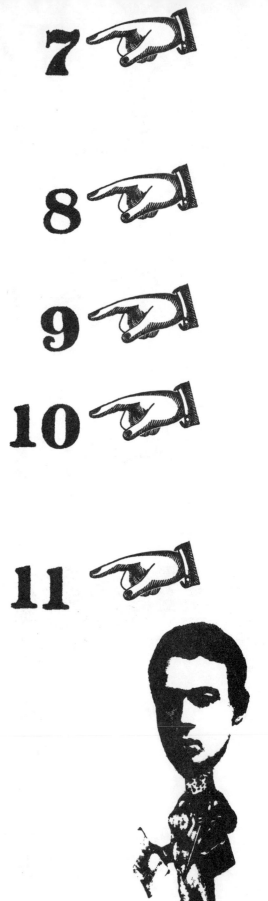

Basic Methods

In the world of ways-to-do-things there seems to be an unlimited number of variations on two fundamental methods:

Perhaps you'll recognize the following basic 'techniques' in your personal behavior.

Trial and Error

The most basic of scientific methods is known by all as 'trial and error.' If at first you don't succeed, try and try again. Trial and Error is the seed that breeds hundreds of simple and complex offspring.

Checklists

List-making has many variations including checklists, lists of components or parts, lists of purposes and reasons, lists of options and possibilities, lists of cautions and fears, lists of things to do, etc., etc. Brainstorming, possibly the most popular among consciously applied design methods, is a list-making technique.

Learning to make lists is fundamental to becoming more methodical and process-aware. Shopping lists and other daily "to-do" lists are good places to begin. Become a better list-maker and you'll be on your way to more successful (creative) problem-solving.

There are no limits at the outset of solving any problem or turning any dream into reality. Everything about the 'situation' is open-ended.

Process Specific Methods

Like Nature with its dynamic changing seasons, nothing is static about creative problem-solving. The dynamic alternation between convergent and divergent thinking involved in the following sequence of generic methods is a 'natural' progression. Conscious 'focus' on any detail of a 'big picture' requires that you first broaden your scope to see the whole, then narrow down to see the parts.

ACCEPTANCE

The start of any eventually satisfying journey is a willingness to go. I'LL BUY THAT is the basic method. It requires assigning a percentage of your assets to a particular activity; narrowing (converging) choices from everything potentially possible to the few that are realistically doable. How you get started is a personal matter. Knowing what drives you to accept a challenge and become involved becomes all-important to success. Reward moves some; some depend on threat. Which will it be - a carrot or a whip?

ANALYSIS

The basic method is WHAT'S INVOLVED? Before you can develop an understanding of any situation, you need to get the facts. Often cloaked within the fuzzy issues of initial problem statements, you'll need to apply some variation of this method to uncover them.
Finding facts and how they interrelate requires searching for related information...questioning all sides of the situation...examining the details...involvement in fair and impartial, open-minded research. (Divergence)

DEFINITION

The basic method is ESSENCE-FINDING. This convergence method involves the digesting of information to reveal "essential" guidelines. When boiled down to the important aspects or interrelationships, those "essences" allow you to formulate a "concept" or basis for further options, decisions and actions. Once identified, the essential ingredient(s) provides direction to a successful conclusion. This key stage often requires forming an attitude or taking a stand.

IDEATION

The next basic step, a divergent phase, is IDEA-FINDING; the search for all possible "means" to translate definitions to reality. The task is to develop a spectrum of choices or "options." Finding ideas depends on your ability to widen your thinking from the narrowed definitive stage that came before it. Deferring judgment until a sufficient number of options is generated is all-important at this phase.

IDEA-SELECTION

The basic method, THE BEST WAY, entails comparing what you want with what you can have. From analysis you uncovered the facts. From facts you determined essence. With ideation, a variety of ways (options) to realize that essence was revealed. Where before, ideas were without clear purpose, they are now more or less meaningful in terms of the 'definitions' stated. What remains is to decide (converge) which of those "ways" will best do the job.

IMPLEMENTATION

MAKE IT REAL!, the next basic method, is another divergent experience. It evokes action by formulating plans and translating abstract 'virtual' thoughts and words into concrete reality. It's almost like returning to "Go" except you now know where you're headed and the path you plan to take. Making it happen can entail many more decisions. It is here where sub-problems are most likely to occur and where beginning problem-solvers often lose sight of the stages in the process that led them this far...almost to the end.

EVALUATION

For the final convergent stage of the process, the basic method is HOW'D I DO? Since evaluation involves comparing aims and intentions with attainment and achievement, it is here where plans for improvement are formulated. But why wait until the end to check on progress when ongoing evaluation can serve as both guide and travel companion throughout the journey? ACCEPTANCE is the logical initial Design or

which specific situation bothers you ?

Introduction to ACCEPTANCE

Relax and enjoy it!

Creative Problem-Solving Stage on a creative problem-solving journey. Although enjoying a trip and having some learning rub off in the process are possible without full acceptance on your part it should be clear that deeper learning and greater pleasure can only be gotten via whole-hearted involvement.

To ACCEPT is make something part of your life... to open yourself to it...to assume involvement. Acceptance is a voluntary agreement to adapt yourself and your needs, at least in part or for a trial period, to something else. In short, ACCEPTANCE IS AN ACT OF SELF-GIVING. As such, it makes sense to consider carefully what you can feasibly accept or must practically reject in life. Getting in over your head or never getting involved are the extreme fringes of poor acceptance management.

Being conscious of acceptance can help you determine whether or not you have the time, resources, ability, and energy to tackle a new situation... to determine whether or not you should be or even could be involved... to see if it does or does not fit into your existing schedule of priorities.

Since it's more difficult to "back out of" a situation than to "rush into" it this first 'stopover' involves some self-knowledge to be meaningfully experienced. Success demands that you get moving and remain involved. Knowing your limits and your potentials will be key to your development of self-motivation.

DEPTH OF INVOLVEMENT is the best measure of ACCEPTANCE. Involvement comes in varying degrees. Some problems, because they are obviously more important than others, demand undivided attention. Others may only need partial attention and therefore require less effort on your part. It is possible to accept many situations concurrently. But when your energy and attention are divided among too many situations, involvement in at least some of them will diminish. Students taking a heavy load of varied courses often begin with the best intention to give each separate subject their full focus only to suffer from the illogic of their scheme at the end.

Plan to ACCEPT whatever you undertake so that your involvement will be seen in the results. Beware of accepting more than is physically possible at any one time.

Language Guide For Acceptance

Sincere involvement is clear when both problem and problem-solver become harmonious, as though one.

To accept a problem situation is often stated as:

...to state initial objectives
...to "buy" the situation or need
...to concede or give in to the situation
...to assign autonomy to the problem; to give it life
...to assume responsibility
...to re-dedicate your time and energy
...to believe in the problem; become its advocate
...to pledge one's self to the problem
...to make a contract
...to agree, consent, or approve
...to become wedded to the situation
...to relate personally
...to establish motives; become motivated
...to get going

What does "to accept the problem" mean to you?

Methods for Acceptance

Since acceptance means to assume the responsibility for something, before signing on to any tour, it's a good idea to see whether or not you have room in your life for one more responsibility. Before intending to spend a chunk of your life solving a problem, you might want to check how that problem relates to your other life objectives and abilities. What follows is a sampling of methods that should help you begin your problem-solving journey with a deeper appreciation for involvement.

ways for getting involved

1. AD VALOREM
2. PERSONAL PRIORITIES MATRIX
3. WHAT'S IN IT FOR ME?
4. SELF-HYPNOTISM
5. CONFORMITY
6. GIVE IT UP
7. WHO IS IN CHARGE?
8. I AM RESPONSIBLE
9. TRAGIC SCENARIO
10. ANALOGY ACCEPTANCE
11. CONTINGENCY MANAGEMENT
12. DECLARATION OF ACCEPTANCE
13. HABIT-MAKER
14. STANISLAVSKI

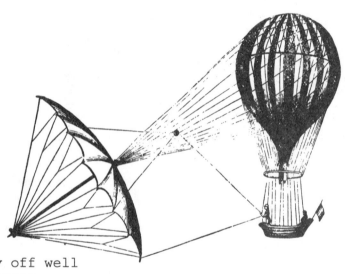

1 AD VALOREM

The best values are those which pay off well in relation to their cost or investment. Among the biggest thrills in life are those where relatively small investments yield huge profits. A smile can earn a lifetime friend. Belief in a cause can help change the world. A notebook or journal that has been personalized with carefully drawn illustrations and relevant notes or details will increase the value of any project or course of study for its owner.

Similarly, effort devoted to solving a problem situation increases in value as the process unfolds and develops.

Two questions continually begging to be answered are: "Is my investment paying off?" and "How can I better direct my efforts to yield greater value?"

Half-hearted acceptance produces half-way solutions.

2 PERSONAL PRIORITIES MATRIX

This method creates an overall graphic model of the entire problematic situation that faces you. It also provides a clue to your expected chances for solving it.

Using a simple matrix or grid of squares you can compare your objectives with your time, energy, and other existing demands facing you.

EXAMPLE:

1. Analyze the situation to estimate its possible costs in money, time, stress, etc. List that information to the left of the horizontal columns of the matrix.
2. Next, list those "given" demands on your time, funds, etc., in the vertical columns of the matrix.
3. Compare the two columns, noting where conflicts appear. Overly conflicting situations suggest that either the problem does not fit your current life-style or that those things currently taking up your time could stand to be altered or eliminated.

Excitement at the outset of a problem is a sign of acceptance. Don't fret. Ride with the feeling.

3 WHAT'S IN IT FOR ME?

How do you expect to benefit from your involvement? How much do you expect to be paid? Make a list of all the benefits that may be gained if you do choose to accept the responsibility for the problem in question. Be as selfish as you like. The truth is that direct benefits such as immediate pleasures, recognition, money, property, and gifts provide more incentive than indirect or deferred payoffs. But in a rush for easy profit just don't forget to include those intangibles such as improvement of skills and general attitudes and gaining new knowledge, items which could be highly valuable for other situations in life. In the end the combined benefits should outweigh the costs to you in order to make your investment of energy worth your effort.

If you do choose to accept the problem, you may want to carry your "payment" schedule along with you. It will be a constant reminder to persist if or when the going gets tough.

Acceptance demands adaptability, tolerance and self-motivation and most of all, freedom from fear of failure.

4 SELF-HYPNOTISM

This is a method for talking yourself into and through a problem-solving situation. Go to a quiet place. Take a walk alone or shut out the world of people and problems in some way. Clear your mind of everything. Try to shake off all awareness of your environment. Focus on relaxing your limbs and muscles. Your body should feel first heavy, then numb, and then asleep. Don't allow anything to distract you from clearing your mental screen.

When you are relaxed and almost on the verge of sleep, slowly fill the void with the positive aspects of the problem situation. Imagine how good it will be when it is solved. Think of how exciting it is to be involved in such an important task and of the feeling of well-being you will accrue as you continue to work at that task. Remind yourself of one of the rewards you expect for solving the problem and enjoy a preview of receiving it. Then, moving very slowly, wake yourself up to the task. The entire process could take as little as five minutes or as long as one hour and can be repeated as often as necessary throughout the course of your problem. (Also see SIDE TRIPS for more on this method.)

5 CONFORMITY

The quickest and easiest way to become a part of something is to become as much as possible like that thing. Conform to the situation and you will begin to exhibit all of the necessary behavior of acceptance. Wear the clothes of the problem; talk its language. Go to its favorite places; eat its food; sing its songs; carry its mottos. Be as much like the problem as you can.

6 GIVE IT UP

Zen philosophy suggests that the attainment of a thing requires the giving up of that thing. This means if you want something you must stop concentrating on having that thing and on the fact that you want it (product orientation) and begin concentrating on what the thing is and on what must be done to get it (process orientation).

"Originality is simply a fresh pair of eyes." Woodrow Wilson

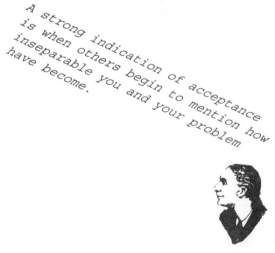

A strong indication of acceptance is when others begin to mention how inseparable you and your problem have become.

40

EXAMPLES

1. If your problem-situation requires you to get $1,000, "give it up." Instead, get involved with things that earn money like turning your hobby into a profit or getting into some money-producing interest. By thus "giving it up," you will probably end up with more than the mere $1,000 you had as an initial product intention or goal.

2. If your problem is to design a house, "give it up." Get into what makes a house satisfying and you will soon be designing a good house.

7 WHO IS IN CHARGE?

The most profound choice in life is to either accept things as they exist or to accept the responsibility for changing them. We all control our own environments in accord with our decision. The moment we recognize a situation in need of improvement we are faced with choosing to live with that shortcoming or to accept the task of improving it.

One method to encourage acceptance, therefore, is to constantly remind yourself of "who's in charge" of your life and to realize that freedom and self-control are only possible for those who accept the task of creating and maintaining their existence.

You might climb the tree, take your arms from around the trunk, and walk out on a limb, but you will never experience flying until you actually let go and jump.

8 I AM RESPONSIBLE

The RESPONSIBILITIES suggested by ordinary problems should seem easy to accept when compared to those connected with running large corporations or governments. To experience how simple it is to carry the load of your problem, try-out for some of those "heavier" roles. Play the parts like a seasoned actor, responding openly to the headaches of some truly tough situation.

9 TRAGIC SCENARIO

One method for developing motivation to solve the situation that faces you is to imagine becoming the victim of all of the worst things that could happen if that situation were not solved.

EXAMPLES:

Suppose you'd like to accept the problem of helping to reduce urban air pollution caused by burning trash and paper in residential fireplaces.

Imagine the worst.1000 new homes have just been built, each with a large fireplace and patio grill. Trash collectors go on strike and every new fireplace becomes a home incinerator for burning trash and garbage. The sky is filled with smog and dirt. Keep on this stream of thought and you will soon build a strong case in your mind for immediate action. The more tragic the consequences imagined, the greater your involvement might become.

It is a mistake to wait until you have a sure-fire solution before declaring your acceptance of solving a problem. With such an attitude you enter problem-solving with all decisions pre-made.

10 ANALOGY ACCEPTANCE

When you have trouble accepting some problem situation, try thinking of ways in which other people or things accept their situations. Through the imagery of the analogy, perhaps you, too, can accept your problem.

EXAMPLE:

How does a toaster accept bread?
It makes it easy by providing a large opening.
It takes it in completely.
It concentrates its energy on surfaces of the toast.
It accepts different sizes and types (within limits).
It follows a programmed setting.

NOW IT'S YOUR TURN!

How does a door accept people?
How does a cat accept affection?
How does a tree accept winter?

Acceptance is like signing a contract to buy an old house. You simply commit yourself to get involved with a lot of work in exchange for the security of having a place of your own.

Note: For fresher viewpoints, select subjects very different from your own.

11 CONTINGENCY MANAGEMENT

Behavior Modification is a well-known and practiced method for changing from one set of habits to another; a way toward managing those barriers that keep you from succeeding or progressing on the path to your goals. From the study of "Behavior Mod" psychologists discovered some basic rules to follow when we find ourselves stymied by the negative inertia of a "contingency" (or unexpected but powerful "reason" that keeps us from moving forward to a goal). Those rules can be paraphrased as follows:

1. BE STRICT and **CONSISTENT**. Don't allow "exceptions."

2. BE REASONABLE and take it slowly. Don't rush in over your head and then have to plead for mercy. Become process-oriented by consciously starting at the beginning and working toward the end.

3. UNDERSTAND YOUR LIMITS. Don't try to do more than is physically possible or probable.

4. PROVIDE INCENTIVE. Make your rewards (or punishments) clear ahead of time... and pay off as you progress. Remember, too, that only short term rewards evoke motivating clout.

Build confidence in your ability to go the required distance. The mere act of beginning a project increases your chances of completing it.

12 DECLARATION OF ACCEPTANCE

It took great courage for the signers of the Declaration of Independence to put their names on a document that subverted their existing government. But their signatures attest to their full acceptance of backing up their beliefs. Perhaps such a document could help you to accept the responsibility of your problem situation.

EXAMPLE:

Write down why you believe that the solving of your problem is important. Write it like a motto, large and clear, and post it near you so that you and others can see it. As a further expression of your commitment, you could Xerox copies and give them to people who you think might be interested.

13 HABIT MAKER

Since acceptance calls for adapting to a new situation, the things that stand between you and your acceptance of change are your habits. It's not easy to change behaviors but the secret is to devote your energy toward starting a new habit instead of struggling to stop an old one. Four standard arguments for resisting acceptance:

1. Avoiding discomfort at any cost...as in weight loss or giving up smoking
2. Finding it easier to do something else...as watching TV instead of studying.
3. Reliance on public opinion...as for tolerating religious or political injustice
4. Overly committed...as when life seems full enough already

Try this: Make a list of the reasons why you are afraid to or merely don't want to face the problem. When done the list will probably reveal or at least hint at some habits that currently make your life comfortable. Then, one by one, consciously attempt to replace them with new more 'accepting' behaviors. Habits don't form overnight. It can take six months or more for a change in behavior to become a way of life.

Acceptance is like signing a contract to buy an old house. You simply commit yourself to get involved with a lot of work in exchange for the security of having a place of your own.

It is a hopeless mistake to wait until you have a sure-fire solution before declaring you acceptance of solving a problem. With such an attitude you enter problem-solving processes with all decision previously made. You will have no alternatives.

14 STANISLAVSKI

Constantin Stanislavski, the Russian director and dramatic coach noted for his teaching of METHOD acting, provides choice advice for becoming "involved." He writes of being "ceremonious," i.e., treating the situation (problem) with reverence and respect. He suggests being "lightheaded and buoyant" regarding the situation as if it had "magical qualities"...of flowing with the situation allowing it to carry you instead of confronting it as something to be manipulated. He suggests dropping all preconcepts or generalized opinions and meeting the situation with a fresh openness and love. It worked for Tom Hanks, Meryl Streep, and hundreds of other famous actors. Perhaps it could help you, too.

Travel Guides for Acceptance

The mere act of beginning a project increases your chances of completing it and builds confidence in your ability to go on to the end.

Ellis, Albert, et al, New American Library (Reissue Ed.)
OVERCOMING PROCRASTINATION

Tracy, Brian, Berrett-Koehler, 2001
EAT THAT FROG! 21 Great Ways to Stop Procrastination and Get More Done in Less Time

Introduction to ANALYSIS

Information obeys no border. Once deep inside of any single thing you begin to find connections to everything.

The next stopover on your problem-solving journey is the convergent, mind-expanding stage of ANALYSIS; the gathering of information. Getting to know more and clarifying all you already know about the problem situation are the two basic tasks. This will be the first test of your ACCEPTANCE, the depth of which will influence the breadth of your analysis.

Since the basic method for ANALYSIS asks the open-ended question, WHAT'S INVOLVED, it is not uncommon to linger in this stage while searching for answers. Information regarding anything automatically extends to everything else. In unfamiliar or complex situations, the time required for information-gathering may actually exceed the total time needed for all of the other stages combined. For simpler or often-encountered problems, analysis may be performed quickly. Estimating a reasonable percentage of your energy to devote to analysis can be a safeguard against using it as an excuse for traveling on.

If you fear that knowing too little about a subject disqualifies you from digging into it, consider the fact that the endless nature of interrelationships makes analysis an endless pursuit; that no one can ever know all about anything. Only reason and limited time can guide you in recognizing when you have gathered sufficient information to proceed to the next stages of the process.

A rich ANALYSIS depends on ample ACCEPTANCE. To be productive at this stage of process, the problem-solver will need to bring along sufficient interest to insure active involvement, energetic curiosity and steady persistence. Before beginning, it would be wise to develop a better perspective for the necessity of gathering information by considering the relationship between ANALYSIS and other process stages.

Language Guide for Analysis

ANALYZING A PROBLEM can be stated as:

BREAKING the problem down to its component parts
RESEARCHING and QUESTIONING
DISCOVERING interrelations and patterns
EXAMINING parts in relation to the whole
DISSECTING or decomposing the problem
GATHERING facts and opinions
GETTING FAMILIAR with the problem
MAKING FRIENDS with the problem
COMPARING a situation with other situations
SHEDDING LIGHT on the problem
SORTING, sequencing or organizing the pieces
CLASSIFYING the elements of the situation
SEARCHING for insight within the problem

WHAT DOES "TO ANALYZE" MEAN TO YOU?

Methods for Analysis

ways for getting to know the problem

1 THE BASIC QUESTIONS

Asking questions, the universal method for finding out about anything, is all that really is necessary for Analysis. However, the desire to determine what, why, where, when, who, or how can be humbling which often calls for courage. Again, giving in to the problem means throwing off fear and pride.

THE BASIC QUESTIONS OF ANALYSIS TEND TO BE:
Where is information to be found?
What is the total scope or "world" of the problem?
Are there experts? Do I know them?
What are my resources and what is required of me?
Which of the limits are fixed? Which can be changed?
Who or what set those limits? When and why?
Do other solutions already exist? Etc.

None are as blind as they who refuse to see. Question and compare with all your senses. Question and compare with all your sense'.

48

Getting to know more about any one thing can become an endless task. Remember that all things are related to everything else. Set a time limit on your analysis phase.

2 THE CLEVER PACK RAT

The Pack Rat, like the crow, for one reason or another, collects anything that attracts its attention. Handled in the style of the Pack Rat, Analysis becomes a random and haphazard thing. To deliberately pursue analysis that way might suggest that logic and energy expense are of no importance. But if time allows, why not gather any information that comes along? What can it hurt?

EXAMPLE: For half an hour each day during the course of your problem, go somewhere new and bring back something new to your problem "nest." Go to a new room in the library, talk with a new consultant, visit an unfamiliar laboratory, observe another problem situation in progress, etc. Don't be too concerned about direct connections or categorization. Just behave like a Pack Rat and bring back anything that "attracts" you. Discovering some relationship between the pieces of your "collection" and your problem situation can become a game after the fact. Remember: All things are interrelated.

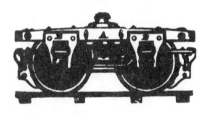

3 SYNECTICS/FORCED RELATIONSHIPS

Gaining deeper insights and new perspectives are both attempts to see things in ways that you have not seen them before. SYNECTICS (also see SIDE TRIPS) and FORCED RELATION-SHIPS are two methods for reaching such new views. SYNECTICS asks, "How is this thing like that thing?" and the result forms a new viewpoint or way to see or understand the subject under analysis.

FORCED RELATIONSHIP asks, "What would result if I combined or joined this thing to that thing?" with conclusions providing deeper insight into the roles of both "components."

EXAMPLE: Analyze a fireplace.
1.How is a fireplace like a breakfast cereal?
They both provide heat by distributing energy.
They are both involved with fuel consumption, etc.

All things are familiar if only you choose to see them that way. Make Analogy-Finding a game. Pick something around you and find ten things that are like it in some way.

4 BACK TO THE SUN

Since all physical things are reducible to
primary energy sources, you can analyze any
of them by tracing their "history" to the
basic natural source, the Sun.

EXAMPLE:
A MEN'S DRESS SHOE

Outer Leather -
Inner lining
and Cushion
Texturing
Coloring
Holes Punched
Die Cutting
Tanning
Slaughter of
animal
Trucking
Animal Breeding
Feed and Grass

Shoe Polish
Coloring
Container
Mixing
Trucking
Chemicals
Petroleum
Fossil
 Deposits

Nails
Hammer
Forge
Wire Spool
Steel
processing
Shipping
Iron
 Deposits

Laces
Plastic Tips
and fibers
Coloring Fiber
Weaving Fiber
Extruding Fiber
Synthesizing Fiber
Plastic
Chemicals
Petroleum
Fossil Deposits

Sole and Heel of
Rubber and Plastics
Stamps
Molds
Heel Factory
Shipping
Raw Latex
Processing Rubber
Rubber Tree
Fossil Deposits

50

5 START A JOURNAL

Sometimes a problem can benefit from having its own 'record book' to separate it from other interests in your life. From the Italian 'giorno' and French 'jour' (day), we derive the English word journal; a daily record. Journal-keeping is a popular way to save facts and discoveries about special interests. This documentary technique lends itself directly to the Analysis Stage of problem-solving, especially when the journal becomes a collection place for comparisons and interrelationships along with facts and data. Many variations of "blank books" are now available for neat journalistic analysis. It's amazing how fast the book fills when used on a daily basis.

6 ATTRIBUTE LISTING

Attributes are those different categories into which the physical, psychological and social characteristics of things can be placed. Getting to know something better involves discovering the special or unique attributes of that thing.

By listing the attributes of any subject being analyzed you gain both general and specific views of the "world" of that subject.

EXAMPLE:

Physical Attributes: color, weight, mass, speed, odor, size, structure, order, etc.
Psychological Attributes: appearance, perceptual stimulus, symbolism, etc.
Social Attributes: group approvals, taboos, responsibilities, politics, etc.
Possible Others: cost, function, durability, ecological connection, time, etc.

Note: Attributes can also be considered as problem variables that are either dependent (on other attributes) or separate. To discern between them may prove helpful in later problem-solving stages when determining essential relationships.

The first question is the hardest, but one question leads easily to another and another.

7 WRITE DOWN ALL YOU KNOW

Most people know much more about things than they give themselves credit for knowing. You may back off when asked what you know about something you imagine not to have examined carefully before, only to discover upon examination that you actually do know much of it. For example, if asked to name 25 different wines, you might balk. Then, after reviewing a list of 50 wine names, you'd probably recognize them all and say, "Oh, I knew those!" But by then it's too late!

This method requires writing down all that you know about the subject in question. You must force it out of yourself, though, because you are naturally reluctant to write down the "obvious." In short, most of what you know is locked inside as potential awaiting your authority for release. Moreover, you'd be surprised at the knowledge two people can recall about a subject by merely "talking it over." Writing the information down or putting it on tape and then writing it down is all-important. Find a pad and pencil and, either alone or with a friend, outline all you already know about your problem situation. Begin with the "obvious." It's probably essential.

8 WHAT OTHERS HAVE DONE

Although revolutionary developments that appear to deny the work involved with process are possible, it is evolutionary growth that is more probable. Both you and your situation are parts of long chains of interrelated situations over time. This commonly used method is based on that fact and deals with the critical examination of solutions that others have applied to solve problems similar to yours.

Again, **MAKE A LIST;** this time your list is of previous solutions. After each entry, include some critical evaluative comments about each one. The library is a good place to begin because most important or ingenious solutions are recorded in magazines, books and professional journals.

A wide-awake young traveler can surpass the overconfident tour leader in the gathering of information about a place.

52

Seek out some of the "dirty jobs" in analysis. Truth often hides in the corners.

9 ANALYSIS MODELS

Another way to get to know about a subject or situation is to make a model of it. Such an abstract "simulation" will help you see the situation more clearly. Models can take many forms. Model trains, airplanes and houses are just one kind of model. They are helpful in visualizing form, color, proportional relationships, etc. But models can be other than three-dimensional miniatures of your intended objectives.

Other ways to model intended objectives include full-size prototypes, charts, statistical graphs, pattern assemblies, biological analogies; perhaps even an ant farm could successfully model a social system, etc. For instance, the best model for analyzing the problem of writing a letter might actually be writing the letter. If it doesn't work out, it's simple enough to start over.

Nothing important will be wasted, and some parts may be reusable if you decide to scrap the first attempt. For more complex problems where people and resources become important, such an approach could get out of hand and quickly become irresponsible. At those times more efficient models would probably be more practical.

"Waking up" to the existence of <u>problems within the problem</u> often comes only after doing it wrong the first time, a bag of different model techniques is handy to carry along on problem-solving journeys.

One kind of model found to be useful in visualizing "whole worlds of potentials" of things is the "morphological" model; a simple technique of organizing the attributes or components of a subject and for dealing with them as interrelationships.

Follow this simple procedure:
1. List all the problem attributes (variables).
2. Categorize the attributes, making separate lists for each category.
3. Systematically determine the combinations by taking one attribute from each list and finding out about that particular combination of parts.

Don't begin your analytic search with a ready-made answer. Use the search to determine the answer. A fixed mind is closed to discovery.

10 MATRIX

A matrix is like the mileage chart found on most road maps. The names of cities are listed in both vertical and horizontal lines at the top and side of a grid. At each intersection of the grid a number that corresponds to the distance between the two cities appears. When a city connects with itself there is a zero or a blank to symbolize "no relationship."

Similarly, a matrix can help clarify relationships between elements or attributes of a problem situation. By placing variables, attributes, or limitations of a problem on both axes of a matrix, you are able to plot the interrelationship between each of them. In this way you can systematically determine which of them are most dependent or independent.

(Note! A numerical rating system can add more precision to this method.) Draw a grid. Place the problem components at both the top and side of the grid and start determining relationships. You will have to work out a system for dealing consistently with all the decisions you must make in the matrix.

11 SEARCH FOR PATTERNS

Within every problem there are smaller problems or sub-situations, and for each of them separate solutions might also be found. Problem-solving often consists of resolving lots of small situations that get you closer to a collective end or goal. Thus, a search for patterns in the sub-situations is another useful method for dealing more knowledgeably with larger issues. Clearly, the more patterns collected, the greater the understanding of the situation under study.

EXAMPLE:

In the problem of how to improve air travel you might uncover the sub-problem of extreme distance between airports and the cities they serve. Workable responses to this situation have been shuttle trains, subways, and helicopter services. This pattern of solutions then becomes a part of a larger language of patterns to be compiled for use in other travel problems.

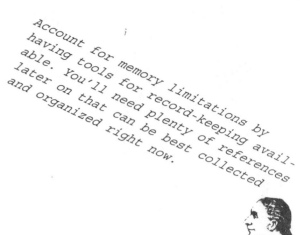

Account for memory limitations by having tools for record-keeping available. You'll need plenty of references later on that can be best collected and organized right now.

Analysis means looking into places you haven't looked before or seeing familiar things in new ways. Going over the same things in the same ways teaches nothing new.

12 THE EXPERT CONSULTANT

When the going gets tough and a problem leans heavily on your back, being able to rely on an expert consultant can save the day. Professional diagnosticians (physicians, lawyers, architects, etc.) suggest that you consider their services as "preventative" measures instead of only when "it's almost too late." This method therefore suggests calling in an expert before, instead of only after, the fact of acting on your problem. The experts you call in may be real or imaginary depending on your time, needs and resources.

TRY THIS: In your mind (or via books, tapes or even reality) call in the one or two people you think would be most helpful to your solution. If your problem deals with religion, you might invoke Allah, Christ, Abraham, or Buddha to sit with you and discuss your situation. They are there, available to serve as your consultants (without charge), if only you choose to ask.

Questioning is a learned skill best developed through practice. Get them out of your head by asking them aloud or writing them down.

13 EXPANDING OBJECTIVES

Problems generally begin somewhat fuzzy and clarify with time and effort. Hopefully, you enter the analytic state by having already accepted certain basic intentions or objectives. As you follow the course outlined by those aims, all new information tends to expand them.

When new discoveries are fed back to clarify basic objectives, those objectives will then guide you into ever new territory as in a chain reaction. In the end, objectives that have been expanded as far as possible become your specifications for the improvements you seek. The more you expand and clarify them, the closer you get to the realization of the solution itself. (See SIDE TRIPS for more on how to clarify objectives by making them "measurable.")

14 THE IDEA-DUMP

Sometimes having an idea early in the game can be your worst enemy, especially if it blocks you from discovering more facets of a problem via analysis.
When you enter into problem solving with 'an ace in the hold' no matter how much you plan to be objective, you already know better than to work too hard at it because at least one solution is predetermined.

The IDEA-DUMP Method suggests that you get your "aces" out on the table from the start so that they won't block your search for more knowledge and perhaps better solutions. Once revealed, those early ideas can be reviewed and add to your understanding of the situation.

EXAMPLE:

1. When entering the Analysis Stage search your mental pockets for 'aces'. Cleanse your mind of solutions.
2. Share your ideas with others. Be critical of them to learn why they could or would not work.
3. Save the usable ideas and parts of ideas for later use if after a more complete analysis, they still prove valid.

The things we lose are often found in unexpected places. If you are looking for information...like anything else, try looking in the unexpected places too.

15 THE SENSITIVITY GAME

If you want to find basic information about a situation, reopen your senses and respond to it as when you were a child. Feel it, taste it, listen to it, smell it. Look at it from many angles. Get close.
Imagination rarely matches reality. As a child, you tended to touch, taste, smell, and listen to everything strange to you. Remember that day when you petted a horse for the first time; how different it was from what your imagination or anxiety had previously led you to expect. Moreover, touching a horse made all the difference in your understanding of horses. That's how you learned what you know in the first place. Normal adults tend to keep their senses under control thus shutting out all new sensory input. But adults who retain their childish sensibilities continue to experience life with 'fresh' eyes and to learn through discovery.

Touch a felt pen to your tongue and at once you become aware of the bitter taste of ink. Pick up a snake to discover it to be less slimy than you thought. Grab a trout from the net and you may find it to be twice as prickly as you imagined. Etc.

16 SQUEEZE AND STRETCH

Just as the wholeness of both convergent and divergent thinking is necessary to the creativity process in general, squeezing and stretching a problem situation becomes a viable method for Analysis.

To see just how much is contained within a situation you have to spread it out. To see its limits and essentials, you have to squeeze it in. In this way you begin to see both the "whole world" of the situation as well as its specifics.

The technique requires <u>a chain of questions</u>. To <u>STRETCH</u> a problem situation and discover its parts, ask a chain of questions beginning with "what."

EXAMPLES
Q. What is the problem about? ANSWER: Judo.
Q. What is "Judo" all about? ANSWER: Physical efficiency.
Q. What is "Physical Efficiency" all about? ANSWER: Finding the optimal use of body movement.

To <u>SQUEEZE</u> a problem down to its essentials, ask a chain of questions beginning with "why."

EXAMPLES
Q. Why am I doing this? ANSWER: I want to.
Q. Why do I want to? ANSWER: It makes me happy.
Q. Why will it make me happy?, etc.

Don't let record-keeping replace reality. If your eye is glued to the camera you may miss seeing the whole scene.

Travel Guides for Analysis

Note: Most of our references from earlier editions are no longer in print. However, some remain available in public libraries or via used book sellers on the Internet.

Gordon, William J. J., Collier
SYNECTICS

Stevens, John O., Real People Press
AWARENESS: Exploring Experimenting Experiencing

Terninko, John, et al, St. Lucie Press, 1998
SYSTEMATIC INNOVATION

And via computer:

INTERNET Search Engines - GOOGLE, DOGPILE, etc.

ENCARTA, an encyclopedic resource for basic data.

Introduction to DEFINITION

*Every country has its own version
of vegetable soup. The names might change but
the ingredients are the same.*

In a logical procedural sequence of events,
the time for getting serious about meaning
has arrived. You've accepted the problem and
analysis is underway. Although probably not
complete, you know much more than before
about the situation at hand. The next leg of
your journey offers the challenge to converge all of those data into an overall intent, into a unified or "definite" statement
reflecting your newly educated understanding. The task is to find the best words for
translating your thoughts into a verbal-
visual banner of understanding; your guide
to moving forward to intentional goals and
objectives.

In life as well as on any problem-solving
journey, the search for meaning or understanding is constant and never-ending. "What
does it really mean?" you ask. "What is really going on here?" "What truly is the
heart of the problem?" You begin every trip
at one level of understanding and end at
another level.

Since meanings are perceptions of reality,
most are retained as thoughts rather than
words. The creative problem-solver translates thinking into knowing by going a step
further with the help of words. But words
have their own limitations. Words are merely
symbols for meaning. When you choose words
to convey your meanings, you are sometimes
understood and sometimes not. When it comes
to Definition, dictionaries aren't much help
because they **do not define** words. They
merely list word usage, i.e., the ways that
people use words to convey their perceived
meanings. Unabridged dictionaries, for example, offer many different usages for
words. When you 'define' something using
words, the particular usage you select is
the one that most clearly reflects what you
intend to communicate; i.e., the one that
best says what you mean. Another person may

choose another usage of the same words to reflect a quite different meaning. It is those differences in meaning that establish our special personalities and potentials and allow us to remain apart from one another within large societies.

With definition you are building a bridge between what you have discovered about a situation (ANALYSIS) and what must be accomplished to resolve it (SYNTHESIS).

For the remainder of your journey, the 'bridge' of definition will act as a filter, allowing you to judge and separate what is relevant from everything else. It will serve as your guide when generating options and developing criteria for choosing from among them. It will be the "stand" you take, the expression of your understanding, the translation of your intention or meaning: your "concept".

Language Guide for Definition

A DEFINITION CAN BE STATED AS:

...analysis in a nutshell
...a motto or directive
...a statement of essence or unifying concept
...an outline for action
...a distillation of research
...the translation of facts into guidelines
...an overall goal
...specification of intent
...a declaration of attitudes and intentions
...an educated viewpoint

OTHER SYNONYMS USED TO EXPRESS DEFINITION

...description
...statement of clarity
...explanation
...characterization
...sense of the matter
...gist, nut, kernel, heart
...significance; implications

DEFINITION
is the
BRIDGE
between
Analysis & Synthesis

Methods for Definition

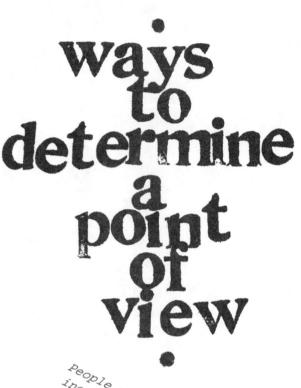

ways to determine a point of view

1 POINTS OF VIEW

If you know how others, especially those involved, feel about a particular situation, you are in a better position to determine how to feel about it yourself.
List those groups or persons or living things who you expect will be affected by your view. Then, trying your best to see the situation through their eyes, write down their probable concerns. Finally, decide, as objectively as possible, which of those concerns or points of view should be included in your own problem definition.

People use words to express meaning. Words don't have meaning. Only people have meanings.

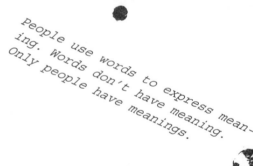

2 ESSENCE-FINDING CHART

In a simple chart of relationships, all of the attributes or components of a problem can be rated according to their degree of dependence upon or independence from one another. By comparing them, one at a time, against each other you can better determine their degree of interdependence within the whole group. In this way the key or essential elements can be determined.
Situations containing vast numbers of components can become quite difficult to manipulate requiring neat grids or matrices and strict adherence to notation and consistent criteria. Computer assistance might be required in very complex or very important situations.

The basic definition-triggering question is "What is the real problem?" It may have to be asked many times before a relevant response occurs.

*Weather Forecast:
Early fog will lead to clear
skies and sunshine.*

*If you can't seem to arrive at a
meaningful Definition, it's possible that you missed the boat
when it left Analysis.*

*Think ahead. Stating clear, complete,
definitive objectives now can avoid
headaches when making choices and
evaluations later on.*

3 "HAPPINESS IS"

Charles Schulz suggested another useful definitive tool with his cartoon book titled
HAPPINESS IS... Trying to manufacture many
"definitions" for one thought will force you
to expand your initial understanding of that
thought (or situation).

Write your current definition of the problem
at hand on a blackboard or sheet of paper.
Beneath it, write as many words as you can
to 'further' define it. When you run out of
words, ask others to join in. Leave writing
tools near the list to encourage them to add
definitions from time to time while you are
involved in other aspects of your research.
You might enlist greater involvement by
treating it as a graffiti game, allowing
anyone to add anything that might occur to
them. It shouldn't take long to amass a collection that just may contain insight previously missed.

4 KING OF THE MOUNTAIN

In the children's game called KING OF THE
MOUNTAIN, one player climbs on top of something, claims ownership, and the others try
to take it over. Each unsuccessful attempt
to unseat the "king" strengthens his position. After a series of takeovers or failures, the relative strengths of players are
revealed.

Following the same concept, the elements,
components, objectives, and attributes of
problems can be played against one another
to determine their hierarchy of importance.
By adding their total number of wins or
losses, you can better decide on the ones
which are the strongest over all others.

For a variation, try teaming two players
against other teams of two. Play until every
pair has played against every other pair to
determine the winning pair of definitions
which should represent the "essence" or
heart of the situation as you now see it.
Definitions are generally personal and subjective points of view. Don't expect your
definition to be whole-heartedly accepted by
everyone.

63

5 KEY WORD DISTILLERY

This is a deductive method by which a series of disjointed aims can be distilled into unified objectives. It entails writing a statement that describes the key issues and aims of the problem as you see it, then extracting the key words or essentials to create a more concise statement.

DIRECTIONS:

Work alone or with a group to prepare a statement of what you believe to be important about the problem. In it, describe the major concerns and objectives; i.e. what you feel is important and/or clearly relevant to a successful resolution of the overall situation. Stop only when you are satisfied that the statement describes the problem clearly and broadly.

Then go through the statement word by word, encircling all words and phrases that appear more important or essential than others. Next, using only those key words and phrases, prepare a second statement; now you have a closer approximation of your problem definition. It may be necessary to rearrange the key words several times until their essential meaning becomes clear.

Definitions are generally personal and subjective points of view. Don't expect your definition to be wholeheartedly accepted by everyone.

The basic secret of solving a problem is to erect a bridge of definition between the way things are and the way you want them to become.

6 PROBLEMS WITHIN PROBLEMS

Trying to improve teaches that inside of every problem situation many sub-situations can be found. Locating and resolving the key sub-problem from among them is another way to uncover a previously unseen 'essential' ingredient. Locate and solve the most critical sub-problem and thereby solve the entire situation. (See also Analysis: Search for Patterns)

A definition may sound amateurish or strange at first. But, expertise doesn't "just happen." It develops.

Definitions are often quite different after analysis than they were before it. Increased knowledge has a way of changing things.

7 TALK IT OUT

"Two heads are better than one" is the basis for this method which simply suggests that definitions come easier when you sit with a friend or consultant and "talk it out." You can attempt to discover, through discussion, what you agree upon as being the core of the situation. It's amazing to see how many definitions can be talked out of situations that seemed complex and befuddling only minutes before when the problem was yours alone. Others will usually join in since it is easier to deal with a situation where the responsibility has been accepted and assumed by someone else.

8 PARAPHRASE

Saying the same thing many ways is a proven technique for expanding familiarity and gaining insight. To find new and different words each time forces a change in perspective and viewpoint. The result is a deeper understanding or definitive view.
Using the knowledge gained during Analysis, write out a statement of Definition as best you can. Then, <u>trying to not use the same words twice</u>, rewrite the statement several more times.

Travel Guides for Definition

<u>Baron</u>, Jonathon, Cambridge Univ. Press, 2001 THINKING AND DECIDING

<u>Hammond</u>, John S., et al, Harvard Bus. Sch. Press, 1998 SMART CHOICES

<u>Oesterle</u>, John A., Prentice Hall, 2nd Ed.,1997 LOGIC: THE ART OF DEFINING AND REASONING

Introduction to IDEATION

Having many ideas improves your chance for having one good idea.

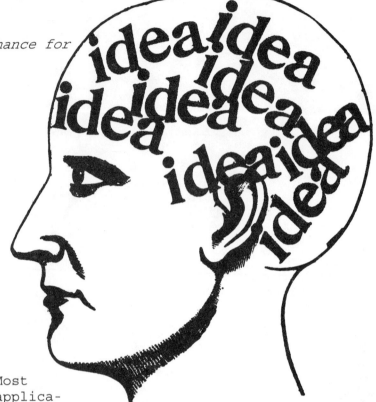

Sharing ideas is everyone's game. Most people have lots of ideas and few applications. An idea isn't much help to you if your objectives are poorly defined. Taken out of context ideas are mere thoughts without purpose.

Having specified a destination by defining the problem now puts you in a position to seek many different ways to get there. To search for those 'different ways' or options is called IDEATION.

Ideas aren't always 'new' or inventive. It's painful, but common, to see someone struggling to find a "new idea" when getting lots of ideas is really easy. Using only a few idea-generating methods, a skilled problem-solver can manufacture great quantities of ideas quickly. And, with many to choose from, one 'good idea' will surely be among them...perhaps even something 'new'.

Language Guide for Ideation

The more ideas you gather, the better are your odds for having good ideas.

Be wary of accepting an attractive idea too soon. You might take a trip to a destination other than your own.

IDEATION
can be stated in a variety of ways:
...Generating alternate routes
...Finding the ways or means for reaching goals
...Outlining various strategies for achiev- ing objectives
...Listing options or alternatives
...Uncovering possible choices for action
...Dreaming of different ways to do some- thing
...Checking out potential plans for resolv- ing a problem
...Inventing
...Brainstorming

What does ideation mean to you?

WATCH OUT FOR A CHANGE OF MEANING
Because the word "idea" is so often used in conversation it is not uncommon to hear it used to convey various meanings. The most common meanings are:
'alternative' as in...
...This is the best idea (alternative) of all.
Or
'thinking' as in...
...My idea (thinking) is to take the day off.
Or
'method' as in...
...The idea (method) of swimming is as easy as 1-2-3.
Or
'invention' as in...
...Edison was America's greatest idea man (inventor).

Methods for Ideation

1. BRAINSTORMING
2. MANIPULATIVE VERBS
3. SYNECTICS (ALSO SEE SIDE TRIPS)
4. TELL ME, STRANGER
5. GO TO THE LIBRARY (OR TO THE INTERNET)
6. ATTRIBUTE ANALOGY CHAINS
7. GET OUT OF TOWN
8. FORCED CONNECTIONS MORPHOLOGY
9. SEEDS OF IDEAS

1 BRAINSTORMING

Asking a leading-question and following a few basic rules are essential to finding ideas. If you want lots of ideas you've got to ask a question that begs for lots of ideas such as... "What are all the ways to...?"

BRAINSTORMING is the universal idea-generating method. You will find it useful in all stages of the design or problem-solving process. Any individual or group of two to twelve persons can quickly manufacture scores of ideas for any problem situation in very short periods of time. Fifty ideas in five minutes is normal production for a beginner group obeying the four essential rules.

OFFICIAL RULES
(See Osborn, Applied Imagination)

1. DEFER JUDGMENT. (No criticism allowed. Judgment comes later, not now.)
2. FREE-WHEEL. (Stay free and loose; allow anything to happen. No action is being taken.)
3. TAG ON. (Right now everything is public domain. Make more from what you or anyone has already said.)
4. QUANTITY IS WANTED. (Work hard and fast. Don't stop.)
   Note: When the rules are forgotten or ignored production is automatically retarded.

Suggestions: 1. Start with a small group before going it alone. Rules are easier to remember and translate into your behavior

ways to broaden the field of choice

that way. 2. Limit sessions to five minutes maximum. If the rules are being followed, you'll be worn out by then. 3. Plan a follow-up session the next day to collect "after-thoughts."

2 MANIPULATIVE VERBS

Still another Alex Osborn method uses a series of verbs (action words) to help visualize a subject in new or unique ways. Verbs suggest manipulation, such as changing position or altering shape, function, size, etc. MANIPULATIVE VERBS can produce a series of ideas in a short time.

Osborn's verbs are MAGNIFY, MINIFY, REARRANGE, ALTER, ADAPT, MODIFY, SUBSTITUTE, REVERSE and COMBINE.

Using them to generate ideas for "improving family relations," you might manipulate the word 'family' as follows:

MAGNIFY - Many different persons in one group; a commune, a neighborhood, a school
MINIFY - A one person family; every member plays all the roles
REARRANGE - Children assume parental responsibilities while parents play
ALTER - Adopted members change all interrelationships
MODIFY - Members rotate roles according to schedule
SUBSTITUTE - Two mothers instead of father/mother
REVERSE - Children choose parents
COMBINE - Family members become business partners

Expanding Osborn's list, OTHER verbs might also be used to produce unique ideas:

Multiply	Distort	Fluff-up	Extrude
Divide	Rotate	By-pass	Repel
Eliminate	Flatten	Add	Protect
		and	

Subdue, Squeeze, Subtract, Segregate, Invert, Complement, Lighten, Integrate, Separate, Submerge, Repeat, Symbolize, Transpose, Freeze, Thicken, Abstract, Unify, Soften, Stretch, Dissect

Can you think of five (5) more?

SYNECTICS

More than a method, Synectics is a process that combines several of these methods. It can be used to generate fresh definitions as well as ideas. (See SIDE TRIPS for a complete description.)

4 TELL ME, STRANGER

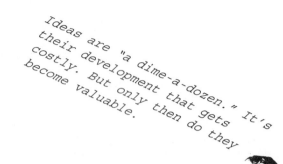

The problems easiest to solve usually belong to someone else. When a problem becomes "your problem," psychological barriers suddenly appear to make it seem more complex than before.

Following that line of thinking, you might benefit by asking someone else for ideas. Since your problem is not theirs, they may have many ideas for you. The more casual the acquaintance, the more likely it will be that you will be given a unique view. Because they assume nearly the same personal feeling toward your problem as you do, close friends are often useless for such advice.

EXAMPLE:
Imagine that you are a biologist trying to solve a problem of regenerating marine life in tide pools. You have defined your problem, stated your objectives, and now need ideas for taking action.

METHOD:
Ask a sociologist. Ask an ecologist. Leave your lab and ask the first five (5) people you meet. Write down all of their ideas, and bring them back to be considered as potential variations.

5 GO TO THE LIBRARY (OR TO THE INTERNET)

Accounts of how problems like yours have been solved in the past are stored in libraries and Internet archives. "How to do it" books, magazines on current techniques and many points of view regarding your situation are available to you. A Reference Librarian or Web Browser can uncover piles of information on ways of doing things as well as suggestions for other idea-spurring materials. If you record all ideas and seeds of ideas as you go, a long list of alternatives will soon develop.

6 ATTRIBUTE ANALOGY CHAINS

Like most things in life, ideas flow easily once inertia is overcome. A proven inertia-breaker is the use of analogy whereby one thing leads to another.

METHOD:
1. Go back to analysis and recall the various physical, functional, social, etc., attributes of your subject (See Attribute-Listing, Analysis Method No.6)
2. Find analogies for each attribute.
3. Build new ideas from the results.

EXAMPLE: FIREPLACE:
Several attributes are:
Materials: brick, stone, steel, cast iron, adobe
Function: provide heat, psychological warmth, decoration, sculpture, structural strength
Fuels: wood, coal, charcoal, paper, gas, solar

IDEAS formed from connected attributes:
Materials: bricks of iron, cast clay ovens, stones of steel (stamped sheet metal), paper stone (asbestos entrained inside clay), cast heat-proof glass
Functions: cook on the hearth, "hearth warmer," wall of fire, fireplace becomes solar furnace (focuses sun's rays), fireplace as heat emitting sculpture
Fuels: coal made of paper, twice-burning composites as in wood becomes charcoal, coal becomes gas, etc.

7 GET OUT OF TOWN

Although discoveries can be made without leaving your own chair, getting away to a new environment is the standard way of developing new points of view. If you were attempting to solve the problem of polluted air in Los Angeles you might get out of town (at least in your imagination) to Tokyo, Sao Paulo, Ankara or London to see how it is being dealt with in those places.

Inventions are but new ways for combining old bits and pieces. New ideas are rare. If you are first to find one you will suddenly be all alone.

8 FORCED CONNECTIONS MORPHOLOGY

This is a technique for generating unique ideas which, when developed, can become inventions. Remembering that inventions are merely new ways of combining old bits and pieces, forcing connections between parts in a morphological listing can produce a myriad of unique combinations.

1. In columns, side by side, list the attributes of the subject under study.
2. After each attribute, list as many alternatives for that attribute as you can. (Brainstorming will help here.)
3. When your lists are sizable, make random passes horizontally and laterally through them, taking one item from each row and force-combining them into new relationships.

EXAMPLE: Generate an idea for a unique ballpoint advertising pen.

SOME ATTRIBUTES OF EXISTING PENS:

FORM	MATERIAL	INK	AD TYPE & LOCATION
CYLINDRICAL	PLASTIC	COLORED	ON SURFACE
FACETED	WOOD	CARTRIDGE	INSIDE
SPHERICAL	METAL	SOLID	ON CAP
CUBE	GLASS	LIQUID	EMBOSSED
DOUBLE-DUTY	PAPER	ERASABLE	ENGRAVED
FLAT	COMPOSITE	PERMANENT	ON POCKET CLIP

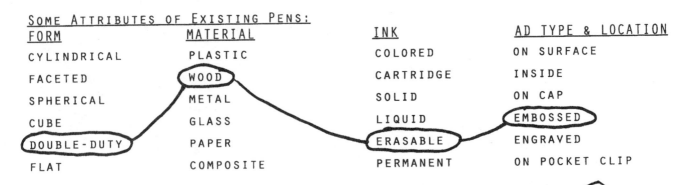

Resulting INVENTION:
Connecting the attributes double-duty form, wood material, erasable ink, and embossed printing, you might envision a pen similar to a carpenter's pencil which also serves as a ruler with advertisement.

With this method, nearly endless combinations of a given number of parts can be found, such as plots for a TV series, curricula for study, automobiles or appliance models.

9 SEEDS OF IDEAS

To find an idea is to have only one. To find the source of ideas is to have discovered the potential for many.

Instead of looking for "one way out" of every situation, it might be more useful in the long run to search for the seeds or principles of ideas that might then be applied over and over again to a variety of problem situations.

METHOD:
1. Analyze your situation to find the possible principles involved.
2. Apply one of the principles or one of its known variations to your idea-finding task.
3. Use the ideas and save the principle for similar future situations.

EXAMPLE:
The physical principle <u>reduce friction to increase</u> efficiency derived from using motor oil can be applied across the board in dozens of problem situations, i.e.,
<u>Phone callers intrude on study privacy</u>
Reduce friction by turning the phone off, installing an answering device, studying where there is no phone.
<u>Freeway traffic reduces the pleasure of driving to work</u>
Reduce friction by taking the train, bus, bicycle, or walking or driving only on side streets, working closer to home, moving closer to work.

Ideas are "a dime-a-dozen." It's their development that gets costly. But only then do they become valuable.

Inventions are but new ways for combining old bits and pieces. New ideas are rare. If you are first to find one you will suddenly be all alone.

Travel Guides for Ideation

<u>Baron</u>, Jonathon, Cambridge Univ. Press, 2001
THINKING AND DECIDING

<u>Burns</u>, Marilyn, Weston, Martha., Little, Brown & Co. THE BOOK OF THINK

<u>DeBono</u>, Edward, Little, Brown and Co., 1999
SIX THINKING HATS

<u>Wujec</u>, Tom, Main Street Books, 1995
FIVE STAR MIND: Games and Exercises to Stimulate Your Creativity and Imagination

Introduction to IDEA-SELECTION

It makes little difference where ideas come from; it's what you do with them that matters.

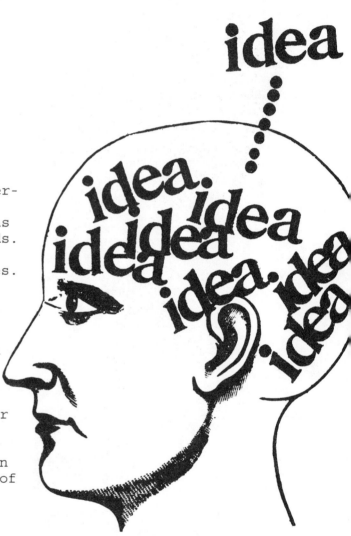

Difficulty with decision-making is a universal problem. The causes: fuzzy goals, unclear objectives or purposes, lack of ideas and lack of familiarity with simple methods. However, for you such normalcy should not interfere with your ability to make choices. As a creative problem-solver, aware of design process and basic methodology, decision-making should be easy.

If by now you have accepted, analyzed, and defined a problem, and have generated dozens of possible ways to turn your definition into reality, the next step is to decide which idea is the 'best'. If your definitions and/or objectives are clearly stated in measurable terms, i.e., you know with some degree of precision what you mean by the term 'best', it is merely a matter of comparing your definitions with your ideas to determine which ideas seem 'most likely to succeed'. The 'best' one(s) will automatically stand out. It's that simple.

CAUTION: Decision-making requires maturity. To choose one means leaving the others behind...at least for now. Sometimes an idea can get you off-track and away from your goals by offering possibilities not included in your stated intentions. Don't stick to an original objective if a new idea suggests that changing it might produce better results. You made the original statement. Who is better able to make revisions? When problem definitions get put to the test, there are still three choices: revise them, replace them, or follow them.

Language Guide for Idea-Selection

A foreign language is simply a different set of symbols for the same reality that confronts everyone.

To **SELECT IDEAS** is often stated as

...deciding on the way that best suits the purpose

...comparing desires with choices

...choosing the most promising path to a destination

...narrowing choices from many to one (or a few)

...committing to a particular course of action

...making up your mind

Methods for Idea-Selection

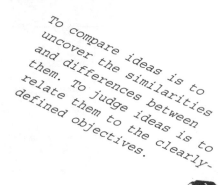

To compare ideas is to uncover the similarities and differences between them. To judge ideas is to relate them to the clearly-defined objectives.

1. SCREENING BY PERSONAL OPINION
2. IDEAS—OBJECTIVES COMPARISON
3. POTPOURRI
4. THE INDIAN SCOUT
5. USER-CHOOSER
6. ONE AT A TIME

1 SCREENING BY PERSONAL OPINION

The most common of all decision-making methods is to judge the available options by passing them through the "screen" or test of personal likes and dislikes. It is a technique that calls for stating personal feelings and beliefs regarding the situation under consideration. The common rationale is "I don't need a reason. I just like it and that's all I need to know." It is the creative and process-aware problem-solver who says "I like it because..."

This simple and direct method requires that you compare your choices, one against the other, deciding which one or ones 'seem to' or 'feel like' fulfilling your statement of definition or intention.

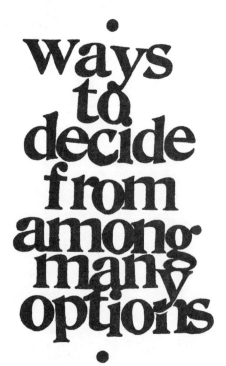

ways to decide from among many options

Unclear objectives lead to un-founded decisions.

2 IDEAS-OBJECTIVES COMPARISON

This technique is a no-nonsense variation on the previous method for making the crucial decision regarding which action to take. It goes like this:

A. REVIEW AND RESTATE YOUR DEFINITION until it becomes the criterion for success. Expand it to become operational by turning goal statements into <u>specific objectives</u>, i.e., actions that must be accomplished for the goal to be reached successfully.

B. RANK AND WEIGH ALL criteria to determine relative importance. Re-list them in order of importance assigning relative numerical values to each entry.

C. CATEGORIZE AND SORT OUT YOUR OPTIONS. Check for repetitions and overlaps so as not to overvalue any single criterion and thus cause it to unduly outweigh others that might be equal. Eliminate duplicates.

D. JUDGE OPTIONS ACCORDING TO YOUR STANDARDS. Group similar ideas so they can be more fairly judged. Use of a grade-point system can ensure consistency of judgment.

3 POTPOURRI

If you can't decide between your options because they all seem to have some specific important advantage that would be a shame to lose, try this:

COMBINE the good points of all the ideas into a new, improved idea not yet on your list.

EXAMPLE: Three ideas for "deriving more enjoyment from my work" are:
Idea 1- Write down the reasons that I chose my line of work in the first place.
Idea 2- Identify happier workmates. Befriend them.
Idea 3- Take a vacation from work and think about it.

Combining all three might be "Turn work into a kind of vacation with enjoyable travel mates."

Note: Instead of trying to have everything at once, it might be better to save some possibilities for another day!

4 THE INDIAN SCOUT

Use of the technique of foresight can improve your chances of avoiding an ambush or other disaster down the line. To better determine what it's going to be like when you actually arrive, get ahead of yourself.

This method is based on the premise that if you use your imagination (or other form of simulated reality) to experience each of your ideas, you will be in a better position to choose between them. The technique tests each idea by asking the question, "What could possibly happen if I actually go this way (carry out this idea to completion)?"

At corporate and governmental levels this method is known as P.E.R.T. (Program Evaluation Review Technique). What is sought is the "critical path"; that particular sequence of events that affects the most important consequences within a total operation.

5 USER-CHOOSER

At times, certain problem-situations warrant the use of outside assistance at the decision-making phase...times when deciding alone would be overly presumptuous and/or manipulative of others or where your lack of experience disqualifies you from taking total charge.

When others are included, you can help them to better understand the problem by organizing the existing requirements (defined criteria) and the options being considered in such a way as to eliminate confusion and facilitate their involvement and ultimate value.

To ensure friendly, constructive, thoughtful, and useful advice from others, your choice of helpmates becomes critical. Offhand, negative input from ill-chosen advisors can send both you and your project into a tailspin.

6 ONE AT A TIME

The most commonly practiced, and generally least efficient, technique for selecting ideas is trial and error, i.e., physically testing each idea, one by one, before deciding on which ideas are better and which one is 'best'.

Normally appropriate for either detailed scientific laboratory studies in physics and chemistry or for relatively unimportant issues, like choosing flavors in an ice cream shop or 'surfing' offerings on television, a frustrated problem-solver might, if all else fails, resort to this timeworn method.

Trial and Error, although a potentially long, hard, costly, wasteful, and sometimes painful way to decide between many options, can nonetheless produce the answer.

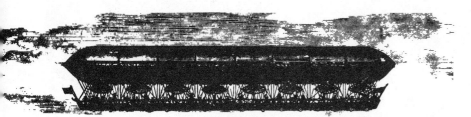

Travel Guides for Idea-Selection

Baron, Jonathon, Cambridge University Press, 2001 THINKING AND DECIDING

Churchman, C. W. , Prentice-Hall
PREDICTION AND OPTIONAL DECISIONS

Hammond, John et al, Harvard Business School
Press SMART CHOICES: A Practical Guide to Making Better Decisions

McCoy, Charles Jr., Prentice Hall, 2002
WHY DIDN'T I THINK OF THAT?

Michalko, Michael, Ten Speed Press, 1991
THINKERTOYS

Russo, J. Edward et al, Doubleday
WINNING DECISIONS

Skinner, David, Probabilistic Publications
INTRODUCTION TO DECISION ANALYSIS

Introduction to IMPLEMENTATION

IMPLEMENTATION is that segment of the problem-solving process where the idea you have chosen as being the one best able to satisfy your intentions is at last put to a test. Implementing your choice is the "moment of truth", the PAY-OFF.

At this stage you should be aware of both the totality and the specifics of a creative problem-solving journey. No longer an awkward tourist with fuzzy plans who would act on random input or impulse, you are now a balanced, knowledgeable and sensitive self-determined traveler.

The time has finally come for you to TAKE ACTION by putting your chosen idea(s) to work. Prepare to enter the tactical, active state of translating your carefully selected idea into the reality of a solution. The foundations have been completed. You are prepared to test your involvement and skills at analysis, definition, idea generation and decision-making. While enjoying the security of having explored many alternatives and concepts along the way, knowing where you are going and why should make the experience pleasurable.

Implementation is best understood as being similar to the 'verb' in a sentence; that part of speech which denotes action. R. Buckminster Fuller, one of the last century's most active creative designers, defined himself when he wrote "I Seem To Be a Verb."

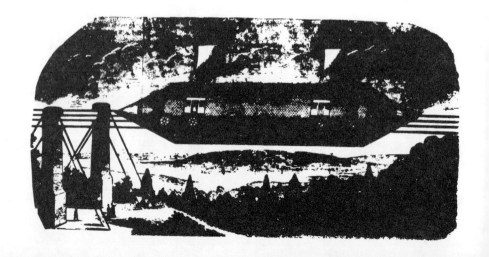

Language Guide for Implementation

Words are symbolic characters and sounds denoting meanings. Words are used to represent reality as perceived by a writer or speaker. They are far from reality but they are the best means we have for objectifying our subjective experiences.

To IMPLEMENT a selected idea is often stated as:

...getting on with it
...putting a plan into effect
...taking action on a chosen idea
...giving form to an idea
...turning an abstraction into concrete reality
...optimizing intentions
...achieving the solution
...realizing or actualizing the concept
...making a dream come true

IMPLEMENTATION can take many forms depending on what you want or plan to achieve:

Acting...Arguing...Administering...Baking...Balancing...
Bicycling...Blocking...Breaking...Building...Buying
Cleaning...Composing...Copying...Cooking...Dancing
Detailing...Digging...Drawing...Driving...Enjoying
Facilitating...Finding...Flying...Grinding...Helping
Inventing...Juggling...Jumping...Kindling...Kissing
Learning...Lecturing...Listing...Milling...Mining
Mourning...Nesting...Nibbling...Organizing...Owning
Painting...Planning...Playing...Quieting...Quilting
Reporting...Risking...Running...Reading...Sculpting
Seeing...Selling...Studying...Spending...Teaching
Testing...Traveling...Visiting...Writing...and
...DOING in lieu of Wishing or Waiting.

Methods for Implementation

1. THE TIME-TASK SCHEDULE
2. BRAINWASHING
3. PERFORMANCE SPECIFICATIONS
4. ADVOCACY
5. LIVE UP TO YOUR NAME
6. DESIGNER'S NOTEBOOK
   A. Diagrams and Schematics
   B. Models
   C. Bionics
   D. Following a Similar Model
   E. Archetypical Form
   F. Common Denominator
   G. Unit Growth
   H. Total Form
   I. Response to Human Needs
   J. Implications
   K. Consultants Team
   L. Structural Limits Method
   M. Sensory Checklist
   N. Role-Playing
   O. Notation Systems
   P. Inspiration or Lightning Bolt

Allow for an occasional "rest stop" to recharge energy and to examine how well things are going.

1 THE TIME-TASK SCHEDULE

In our overcrowded demanding world where lateness is inexcusable and last-minute decisions are only as valid as the quality of process leading up to them, learning to schedule time available with tasks required is prerequisite to success.

1. DECIDE how many and what kind of tasks are involved in performing the requirements for the idea selected. The question: "What are all the steps that must be taken in order to complete this thing?" Specify even small tasks since it is those little things that eventually add up to the total job.

2. DETERMINE THE AMOUNT OF TIME available for the overall project. <u>Don't kid yourself</u>.

3. DISTRIBUTE, as reasonably as possible, portions of the total time to each of the small tasks listed in Step 1.

4. GRAPH the relationship of time to tasks. A wall calendar works well for this step.

5. Allow the TIME-TASK GRAPH to guide you through the implementation phase.

2 BRAINWASHING

Taking action on an idea is not very different from accepting the responsibility for the problem at the outset. The main difference is that in the beginning what lay ahead was unknown. All manner of fears had to be washed away. Although by now you have gone through five (5) phases of a systematic excursion and should be confident, renewing your emotional strength is probably still required for "finishing what you started." You may even have to go back to some of the self-motivation methods from the initial phase of the process to find the courage to go on. You may even have to be reassured of your purpose by reviewing all your work thus far.

Note: BRAINWASHING is a pre-implementation method and is useful in combination with all other implementation methods.

3 PERFORMANCE SPECIFICATIONS

Intentions are transformed into action by breaking them down into small specific steps. In essence, this is a technique for a continual elaboration on a selected idea until it stops being abstract and becomes concrete reality. Once the exact performance you desire is specified bit by bit, all that remains is to translate it into real actions, materials, or other physical forms.

Plan ahead. Before diving right in, try to imagine what it would be like if the journey was already over. The consequences of following a wrong idea could be worse than following no idea at all.

Since "actions speak louder than words," try not screaming with your foot in your mouth.

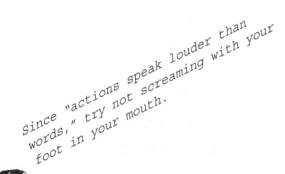

ways for taking action on a decision.

The more that each specific aspect of the chosen idea can be stated in terms of actual planned performance the closer that idea comes to being realized.

EXAMPLE: If the chosen option for improving your life quality had been to move from your dull room and find a livelier, friendlier place to live, SPECIFICATIONS FOR PERFORMANCE might begin like this—
A. Find an apartment near people having interests similar to yours.
B. Look for a place that is known for its parties and social exchange.
C. Swimming pools, saunas, game rooms and a nearby shopping/entertainment center are a must.

Note! When specifications begin to seem redundant, it's a sign for a need to deepen or broaden the scope.

Always carry a few spare ideas along just in case the ones you selected fail without warning.

Implementation can be costly of natural resources. The environment shouldn't pay for your inefficiency or negligence.

4 ADVOCACY

Another way to get an idea going is to help it to help itself. Advocates for an idea can pull it forward while you get behind and push. An architect might help clients become amateur environmental designers and thereby receive "inside help" toward achieving their mutual goals. If the idea selected to implement "achieving a healthier work environment" was "to inaugurate a cigarette and smoke-free day," it can be encouraged to help itself by supporting it with additional bolstering ideas, such as replacing a need for cigarettes with a substitute; offering rewards and penalties for achievers and non-achievers; setting up a mock trial for those caught smoking, etc.

84

5 LIVE UP TO YOUR NAME

Names help you to identify the various people, things, places and events of your experience. Once named, a formerly complex assortment of bits and pieces comes together in your mind as a totality. Similarly, it is possible to begin an active translation of an idea into physical form by finding a name which seems to pull its parts together as a whole and to then give form to the name.

EXAMPLE:
Suppose your plan is to triple the enrollment of a local Eco-Action group and the best idea seems to be 'organizing a recycling party.'
A. Name the event. Let's say you call it "Smashing Good Time."
B. Live up to the name. Have the band call itself the "Can Smashers." Invent a dance called the "Carton Twister." Print invites on can bottoms and tops. Have a can-smashing competition and a bottle-breaking race, etc. It's easy. Once you've got a title, what remains is to merely fill in the blanks.

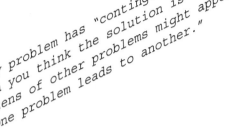

Every problem has "contingencies." Just when you think the solution is near, dozens of other problems might appear. "One problem leads to another."

One person's scheme for improvement will surely become another person's problem.

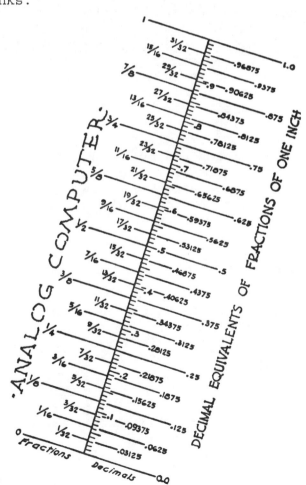

'ANALOG COMPUTER'

DECIMAL EQUIVALENTS OF FRACTIONS OF ONE INCH

Designer's Notebook

6 DESIGNER'S NOTEBOOK

Every cook keeps a recipe file to simplify and facilitate meal-planning. Likewise, active creative problem-solvers (designers) keep a file or notebook of techniques and tricks for dealing with different types of problem situations. Though most of the following methods have been gleaned from the visual design disciplines, it is not unlikely to find them applied by other creative problem-solvers in all areas of human endeavor.

6.a DIAGRAMS AND SCHEMATICS

Designers often begin the implementation phase with scribbled diagrams and schematics to symbolize relationships between the parts of problems. They search, via sketchy organizational diagrams and lists, for the relationships that link the factors and aspects or components of their problem. Such diagrams are called "bubble" diagrams, "flow" charts, layouts, organizational charts, etc. Through repetition and by trial and error, the sketches eventually emerge as refined and definitive relationship drawings to be translated into physical materials.

6.b MODELS

Complex forms and difficult-to-visualize ideas often demand to be "mocked up" to be clearly understood or visualized. The age-old procedure is to begin with physical rough "study" or "sketch" models and work through a series of refinement models until a "finished model" or "working prototype" is developed. Ever-advancing computer modeling adds new dimensions to design visualization and pre-experience of potential solutions.

6.c BIONICS

Being a part of nature and also being able to (mentally) stand apart from nature, it is possible to allow nature to model the behavior of your human intentions.

For every possible idea some natural counterpart can be found. By studying how the natural model works and how it survives or achieves its ends, you will find guidelines for the implementation of your idea.

Bionics, the science of interrelating natural and man-made systems and offspring of cybernetics and biology is still another variation on the MODELS approach. The basic difference is that the bionic model is a natural one.

6.d FOLLOWING A SIMILAR MODEL

Finding problems similar to yours that have been solved to the satisfaction of all concerned is another common technique. You might review how others implemented their solutions and assemble yours in the same way.

This approach, often misjudged as borrowing or stealing from others, is really a form of apprenticeship. When used consciously you express the fact that you are wise enough to build on the experience of others and desire to learn by following a leader.

6.e ARCHETYPICAL FORM

When a child draws lines on paper to represent a house, such a drawing generally represents the stereotypical house; the triangular gable roof shape reflecting the structural archetypes (truss, vault, or frame) that allow it.

Archetypes and stereotypes derived from repeated internal and external forces and pressures acting on a situation become the traditional or original forms of things. From the study of archetypes you learn how to deal with variations and the creation of new forms follows.

6.f COMMON DENOMINATOR

Complex or multi-part ideas may be more easily implemented by locating a common denominator; something inside or beyond the situation that offers a common relationship between all the parts. A familiar example is "modular construction" used by contractors and materials manufacturers to bring all the components of a construction project into dimensional harmony.

Another example: To successfully implement the idea of creating a small community to house families displaced by urban renewal, the common denominator of a mall, shopping district, or Main Street element might be introduced.

6.g UNIT GROWTH

A House of Cards and a "castle" made from children's building blocks are examples of larger things achieved by assembling small typical or identical units and by following a consistent set of "rules" or limits for assembly. In a similar way, other large or apparently complex systems can be constructed. This method begins with a search for an essential unit that can later be assembled in quantity to achieve large and complex "configurations" not easily possible when all parts are allowed to be individually unique. "Small units" grow into larger systems by following determined consistent rules of interconnecting and assembly. The ESSENTIAL UNIT BUILDING BLOCK METHOD can be seen to be a variation of the Common Denominator Method. Still another name for this technique is UNIT GROWTH.

6.h TOTAL FORM

A sculptural or holistic approach, the complement of Unit Growth, is called the Total Form Method. Here you begin with whole assemblages conceived as abstract configurations and proceed to break those wholes down into orderly systems of smaller parts or components. It should be clear that no matter which of the two (Unit Growth or Total Form) methods is chosen, it is not long before the other must also be considered. Since only a few small units may be assembled before it becomes necessary to consider the total form that might emerge, similar attempts to generate whole forms can be taken only so far before attention must be given to the parts and pieces needed to realize the whole.

6.i RESPONSE TO HUMAN NEEDS

All problems in some way begin with unsatisfied human needs and acceptable solutions must eventually satisfy those needs. Today, lists of human needs are readily available to help produce solutions having far more humanistic concerns than before. They generally include the full range of physical needs such as food, rest, shelter, etc., as well as the many psychological needs such as self-respect, friendship, achievement, and orderliness. Ideas being implemented are checked against "needs" on the list and offer response to them.

To use this method, the essence or core of the idea is first reviewed and where possible translated into "needs" terminology. The new 'needs related' statements can be further distilled into an improved definition (essence); a useful tool when evaluating all other apparent results.

6.j IMPLICATIONS

Ideas are abstract statements that imply concrete actions. Otherwise, they're just words. Translating those 'implications' into achievable terms (sometimes referred to as 'objectives') is the first requirement. The leading question is: What types of actions are implied by the idea being considered in the various physical, psychological, social, political, and economical categories?

EXAMPLE: Considering a problem regarding feelings of loneliness, what might be implied by a chosen idea that suggests you should make more friends?
Social implications: Join a group or club; visit more places where people congregate; become interested in the activities of others; buy a season ticket to the Mozart Festival. Etc.

6.k CONSULTANTS TEAM

Become a team leader. Break your idea down into various categories that can be individually acted out by experts. If, for instance, your idea deals with the development of a new product, divide it into the separate areas of market analysis, design, production, advertising, distribution, etc. Arrange to meet the various consultant teams who know each of those areas best. Then, act as the coordinator who resolves all of the opinions of your "expert" staff.

The theory here is that the more people you get in on the act, the better will be the total performance. The dangers are either that the performance will have so many prima donnas it will be difficult to recognize the idea beneath it or that the idea will become separated from its objectives due to one of the experts being stronger than the coordinator.

6.l STRUCTURAL LIMITS METHOD

Every assemblage has a structural framework that holds it together and stabilizes its form. This is as true for music and dance as it is for construction and sports. Moreover, all structures have limits which, if ex-

ceeded, cause failure or collapse of the system. Use of the STRUCTURAL LIMITS METHOD is simply to allow the "structure" or system of forces, loads, stresses and reactions to be the limiting factor.

Begin by identifying the various 'forces' involved within the framework of the problem or its intended idea for solution. Next, assess the importance of each force to determine the necessity for 'give and take' to achieve equilibrium. In the end, when all forces are resolved into an orderly balance, success becomes undeniable.

6.m SENSORY CHECKLIST

To perceive, understand, and hopefully appreciate an idea turned into action, sufficient sensory stimulus must be provided. The perception of reality, being a totally subjective experience, therefore requires that the creative idea implementer provide ample sensory clues to the 'reality' intended; something for the ears to hear, the nose to smell, the fingers or skin to feel, as well as for the eyes to see and perhaps, even for the tongue to taste.

Thus, solutions enhanced by incorporating the five senses as a checklist, become easier for all to appreciate.

6.n ROLE-PLAYING

Role-playing, acting out a potential solution by playing the parts of those affected by it, is a pre-experience technique of living through a scenario of implementation before it actually happens. An added benefit allows for trouble-shooting problems before they occur.
Such 'getting into the act' requires imagination as it helps develop image-making skills. The payoff is in the security gained by having been there before which tends to eliminate fears and anxiety and allow for a more successful solution.

6.o NOTATION SYSTEMS

Like words, numbers and other symbols are regularly devised to simplify the apparently complex problem of dealing with reality. Mathematical and musical notation systems should be already familiar to you. But other

graphic, sonic, or behavioral notations can
be invented quite naturally. A sine curve is
often used to suggest the path of a process,
an arrow can indicate much more than mere
direction. Etc.

When your job requires you to implement
great numbers of similar complex problems,
it may be advantageous to develop your own
notation system.

It can save needless repetition of operations during developmental processes, and
allow you to write or manipulate information
more quickly and thereby keep apace with
your faster thinking ability.

When heading toward any goal, it is no
unusual to cross paths with other goal-
seekers headed in a variety of directions
Stay alert! Avoid collisions by keeping
your eyes on the road.

6.p INSPIRATION OR LIGHTNING BOLT

Some problem-solvers benefit from the age-
old technique of serendipity or simply waiting around for inspiration. They read, talk,
scribble and horse around with their problems and ideas in hope of encouraging a
lightning bolt of inspiration to strike or
for a genie to appear with the wherewithal
to bring their dreams to fruition.

In general, design-by-fate is a poor substitute for goal achievement by conscious orderly process but it can work for you if the
need for a solution is neither urgent nor
important. Since no one can say how "the
cookie will crumble," it might be a reasonable backup plan. This playful method, probably the most untrustworthy of all since it
is highly dependent on factors outside of
your control, is regularly used for "definition" and "ideation" as well as for implementation.

Travel Guide for Implementation

MacKenzie, Kyle, John Wiley & Sons
MAKING IT HAPPEN: A Non-Technical Guide to
Project Management

Possidy, Larry, et al, Crown Publishing,
2002 EXECUTION: The Discipline of Getting
Things Done

Willams, Paul B., American Management Assoc.
(www.amacombooks.org)
GETTING A PROJECT DONE ON TIME

AND

Job Management/ Focused Performance Software
www.workkeeper.com

www.focusedperformance.com

Introduction to EVALUATION

"The world is full of people who know the price of everything and the value of nothing." Oscar Wilde

Goals are moments in time; rest stops in the continuum of life. After reaching a goal, don't forget to look back to determine how far you have traveled and to judge the value of the journey. Measuring success at the end of any problem-solving process is all-important to making future trips run more smoothly. The stage is called Evaluation; a form of accounting. It involves the comparing of actions with consequences; detecting flaws and making improvements; planting the seeds of future challenge.

For any review to be impartial, an honest judgment of performance is required. With an attitude of benefiting from experience, the "honest evaluator" bravely measures both quantity and quality, their sum representing the total "value" received. But being honest with one's self is often anxiety-tempered and certainly not common behavior.
Here is where the importance of clearly stated goals and objectives becomes obvious. If at the outset of your journey you didn't clearly state where it was that you intended to go, it will be difficult, if not impossible, to measure how far you've gone or even whether you've actually arrived.

Evaluation is a link between problem-solving journeys. It not only concludes, it also commences by summing up one journey and preparing you to begin another.

Seasoned travelers know that creative problem-solving journeys are best evaluated without tears when project objectives are clear from the start.

94

Language Guide for Evaluation

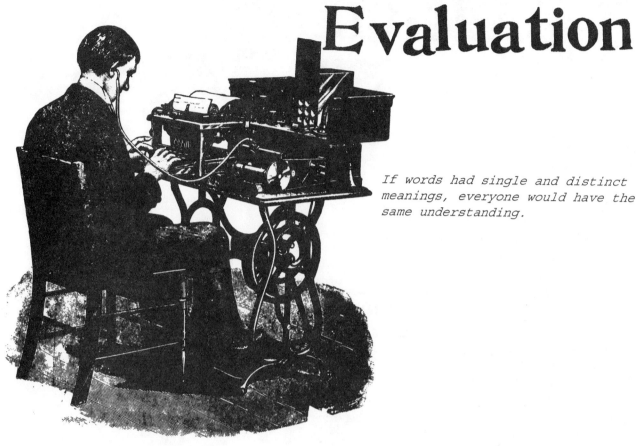

If words had single and distinct meanings, everyone would have the same understanding.

Note: While reviewing your notes to evaluate your travel through the various stages of design process, don't forget the benefit of those minor experiences that might have happened along the way.

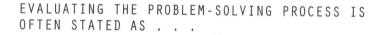

EVALUATING THE PROBLEM-SOLVING PROCESS IS OFTEN STATED AS . . .

...SELF-CRITICIZING; SELF-IMPROVING
...DETERMINING the quantity and quality of achievement
...EXAMINING CHANGES in behavior over time
...GETTING OUTSIDE of yourself for a more objective view of the INSIDE
...DISECTING PROCESS in terms of the PRODUCT
...REVIEWING the past to better determine how to proceed
...TALKING IT OVER
...APPRAISING what has been accomplished
...ASSIGNING VALUE to achievement; grading
...REFLECTING on the past with an eye to the future

What does "to evaluate the process" mean to you?

Methods for Evaluation

1. THREE PHASES OF EVALUATION
2. STEP OUTSIDE FOR A MINUTE
3. WHO ELSE HAS AN OPINION?
4. PROGRESS CHART
5. LETTER TO YOUR BEST FRIEND
6. ACADEMIC METHOD

1 THREE PHASES OF EVALUATION

As for other phases of design process and for life in general Evaluation begins with a question: "What did you hope for and/or plan to happen?" The experience of measuring those aspirations against final accomplishments reveals value received. Gut feelings aside, it is only from such true measurement that the problem-solver learns the quantity and quality of progress and therefore how to plan for future improvement.

GUIDE TO EVALUATION

1. STATEMENT OF GOALS
   Objectives Described in Measurable Terms

2. ACHIEVEMENT AND MEASUREMENT
   A. How far did I go? (quantitative; amount) Number of objectives reached
   B. How well did I do? (qualitative; enrichment)
      Benefits accrued
      Educational: • Knowledge acquired
                    • Skills developed
                    • Attitudes altered
   C. Contingencies
      1. Unforeseen benefits
      2. Unforeseen problems
      3. Additional objectives discovered late in the process
   D. Comparison of Goals with Achievement
      1.   Point by point comparison

3. PLANS FOR THE FUTURE
   A. Review of behavioral modifications

ways to assign value or worth to process

2 STEP OUTSIDE FOR A MINUTE

Making plans and setting out to achieve them
is positive behavior. The relevance, social
value and possible negative consequences of
the success or failure of such behavior is
yet another matter. If your self-image is
good, you know that your intentions are good
and likewise that your behavior is the result of good intentions. When those "good
intentions" are challenged by evaluation,
you may become self-protective and should
take care so as to not be unduly defensive.

Evaluation calls for STEPPING OUTSIDE of our
self-image...at least for a moment at a
time...to look objectively at what transpired. Think of yourself as a Controlling
Spirit that controls a body and its behavior
(yours). Since that Spirit has good intentions, it is concerned with improvement. And
it welcomes the opportunity to observe and
improve the behavior it controls.
The initial attitude of evaluation should be
positive; to make plans for improvement. for
any problem, it requires ACCEPTANCE. When
the evaluator realizes that it is attainment
and not "self" being studied, realistic mea-
surements and improvements can proceed.

3 WHO ELSE HAS AN OPINION?

Being objective about the level and value of
your achievements is tough enough when having to depend on your own subjective position. Others, who view your position with
different perceptions, can often open your
eyes to a truth of reality, which was there
in front of you all the while, but unseen.
To insure that outside opinions are meant to
be constructive and not off-the-cuff or potentially hurtful, they must derive from an
understanding of your situation and your
participation in it. Your job is to do the
explaining.
Some tips for getting an outsider to offer
helpful review:
BE SPECIFIC AND DIRECT. General questions
will only beg general answers.
SUGGEST A REWARD. How can both of you benefit from your experience?
LOOK FOR IMPROVEMENT, NOT APPROVAL. Be convincing that you are serious.

4 PROGRESS CHART

When time is important, an annotated calendar becomes a chart for tracking progress through a process. By making a chart relating your defined objectives (tasks) with your available time, you will also find a simple way to keep a running evaluation. If the chart is kept up-to-date it allows you to see, at a glance, how far along you are in terms of meeting your objectives. This method usually works best for quantitative measures, but quality can be added in the form of side notes or comments as in a journal.

Prejudice is a poor companion on evaluative journeys. It is never too late to change your mind about the value of something.

5 LETTER TO YOUR BEST FRIEND

Another painless way to determine the value of your intentional achievements is to write a letter about them. Simply write as if to a friend or parent (you could easily play the role of your own best friend). Describe your accomplishments and what they mean to you in terms of your initial intentions and how they developed along the way. Tell how valuable they are in both a broad sense and specific sense. You might even mail it for still more feedback... or mail it to yourself to see how it sounds several days from now.

Conscious evaluation anticipates the best possible outcome. It teaches that design is a form of optimism.

6 ACADEMIC METHOD

If you are looking for an age old evaluation method, you'll be sure to find it in school. The subject of grades and grading has been under scrutiny and in use there for centuries. But few students and many teachers appreciate the true potential or intrinsic educational value of its process.

In academic evaluations, letter grades stand for verbal descriptions: A, Superior Attainment of Course Objectives; B, Good or Better than Average Attainment of Course Objectives; C, Acceptable or Average Attainment of Course Objectives; D, Poor or Least Acceptable Attainment of Course Objectives and F, Non-Attainment of Course Objectives. For these symbols to be re-translated back again to evaluative meanings, the "Course Objectives" must be known by both teacher and learner at the outset with the measurement criteria clearly understood by all.

When considered as an evaluative strategy intended for improvement or behavioral change, the process of grading can be far more meaningful than the apparently often misunderstood symbolic letters or numbers that appear on student records.

When course objective are commonly acknowledged by all those who participate, students and teachers become a team working toward mutually understood and agreed ends and fewer unexplained failures occur. Moreover, when objectives are clearly defined self-improvement abounds and it is the students themselves who often become their own best evaluators.

Travel Guides for Evaluation

Brown, Mark Graham, Productivity Inc., 1996
KEEPING SCORE: Using the Right Metrics to Drive World-Class Performance

Harbour, Jerry L., Productivity Inc., 1997
THE BASICS OF PERFORMANCE MEASUREMENT

Questions to ponder...
Answers to find?

If I begin to operate more creatively what changes in behavior can I expect to experience?

• • •

How can my thoughts and feelings be united to make for greater wholeness?

• • •

When one destination is reached, am I at the end of my journey or at the start of another?

• • •

Back home with the memorabilia

Looking back over a completed journey is a mellowing experience. The task of determining the value of process can best be done by viewing the interwoven and diverse behaviors that comprise real life occurring between those brief moments in time called destinations or goals.

For the goal-oriented problem-solver, good times and bad tend to fuse together to become a single memory or general impression. Such general experiences are accented by those most memorable occasions, both the pleasurable and the traumatic, encountered along the way. Minor pleasures, acquisitions, and sub-problems are quickly overshadowed by subsequent fresh experiences. As you lose sight of the details and remember only the major "ports of call," you condition yourself to value only the achievement of the journey without reference to the joy of living the process.

Learning from life experiences requires an appreciation of the interrelationships encountered along the way. If your goal is seen as a product, then process is the path to reach it. But, since you're heading that way anyway, you might as well enjoy the trip.

LIFE IS PROCESS. Living involves going from one activity to another...being procedural. To be conscious of the activities of life is to be aware of life itself. To be concerned for improvement suggests a concern for methodology...developing skill in using the techniques that enhance the enjoyment of process.

PRODUCTS result from PROCESS. Their value derives from an evolutionary series of actions to be re-applied to future process. For example, the product called Graduation is the result of years of study, eating, writing, problem-solving, TV watching, vacations, etc. When graduation finally arrives, it is immediately gone. But the process of living goes on. The day before graduation is little different from the day after graduation; only the process continues with a new set of freedoms and limits.

Documenting an ever-changing process is the best we can do to preserve it. One commonly enjoyed form is the journal, or personal record, of what transpired.

The value of such a documentary product is that it makes process memorable and better able to be valued. It turns experience into an observable and thus improvable thing. For those who solve problems for others, as in a design or consultant activity, documentation of process is part of the responsibility of such professional practice. With a personal evaluative document kept up-to-date, creative problem-solvers will always have a clear view of where they are in relation to the continuing process of life.

SIDE TRIPS

Separating the TRAVELERS from the tourists

Why Side Trips ?

Looking back through a travel journal to evaluate the success of a trip, it generally rests on the depth and quality of the SIDE TRIPS that separate inexperienced tourists from well-seasoned travelers. Similarly, in reviewing creative problem-solving journeys, it is usually the extra-curricular discoveries encountered along the way that determine the most interesting evaluations.

The following Side Trips are offered with the expectation that they might enrich your voyages as they have done for countless other Universal Travelers throughout history.

CREATIVITY GAMES

Results that seem to stem from the conscious application of an unorthodox behavior or unusual method are what most people refer to as being 'creative.' The ability to make and break rules or habits without an undue amount of stress for others is typical of such behavior. In fact creative behavior might be better defined as "behavior that is both subjectively and objectively whole, free from pride and other deadly sins, expressive of constructive discontent and a willingness to succeed, and fearless in the face of rules or habits." Since any change in behavior denotes the breaking of a habit, any game that produces change is a HABIT-BREAKING exercise.

Here are a series of games designed to help with the learning and development of habit-making and habit-breaking.

Games to develop Humor

1 LAUGHTER is an abrupt physical reaction to something "unexpected." Find a cartoon in a magazine and cover up the caption. Then write several captions of your own by changing what might have been "expected" in the drawing to something completely unexpected.

2 MIMICRY, MIME, AND ROLE-PLAYING are all surefire ways to make you smile at your own behavior which is an observable trait of creative persons. Go ahead and try it. Be a Mail Carrier. Be the President. See how close you can come to doing convincing renditions of several movie stars.

3 PUNNING is a favorite activity of most creative persons. They love to find double meanings in various facets of life and they are amused by the often strange relationships they discover in the process. Get with the "groaners" and have some "pun" of your own. It'll free up any tensions you might be feeling and surely bring a smile to your face.

Games to develop

Awareness

1 Try EATING AN APPLE or orange as if you've never eaten one before. Extend all five senses to their fullest appreciative potential. Examine the object slowly and carefully with regard to its shape, color, flaws, textures, flavor, sound-producing quality, odor, temperature, etc. Make lots of analogies as you go, finding image-filled ways to describe the event. Be as poetic as possible.

TAKE YOUR SENSES ON A FIELD TRIP. Go for a walk and concentrate on getting the maximum stimulus for each of your senses in turn. Begin with your skin; feel the temperature differences between one place and another; note where the wind picks up, where heat comes from, etc. Take your time. Then focus on your ears: what sounds?, from where?, what background noises?, what faint hints of sounds from afar?, etc. Take a notebook and document what you discover between each separate sense excursion.

Games to renew the Child in You

1

BI-MODALITY is a recently accepted term for the conscious use of both halves of the brain. One side "knows;" the other "feels." One is the controller; the "adult." The other is the playful child and sensory responder. Here are three exercises to help free the child (whose left brain is probably now working overtime to calculate the possible consequences) in you.

2

IMAGINE THAT YOU CAN JUMP right out of your shoes into someone else's shoes "just like that." Form the image clearly in your head. Practice a few times, stopping between jumps to describe what it felt like to be in one pair, then another, and another. Try at least five such experiences before stopping altogether. What counts here is you agreeing to imagine jumping at all. Left-brainers have big trouble with this.

3

QUICKLY! NO TIME FOR THINKING. Take off your shoes. Examine your toes. Now lie on the floor. Study the ceiling. Close your eyes. Make the sound of a baby chick; chuckle to yourself. Your right brain is active again.

Games to develop Belief in Self

1 WRITE AN ITEM FOR A LOCAL NEWS PAPER describing how well you have solved some important problem situation. Tell about how you were able to achieve what you did. Be laudatory. Describe in detail what a really good person you were (are).

2 DESIGN A MONUMENT TO YOUR DREAMS. What form will it take? Why? Where will it be located? Why? How long should it last? Why?

3 BRAG A LITTLE. Explain to a friend how difficult it is to do what you do but how well you accept your responsibility for doing it despite those difficulties.

4 IMAGINE THAT YOU HAVE JUST WON THE NOBEL PRIZE which brings fame and fortune your way. Now that you are well known and economically secure and no longer need be concerned with those gnawing distractions, imagine how well you can achieve other current goals. Write about it.

5 TRY TO GO A WHOLE WEEK WITHOUT EXPLAINING YOUR ACTIONS OR EXCUSING YOURSELF TO ANYONE. Forget apologies and other humbling practices for this week. Be a little pushy, not aggressive and hurtful, but assertive of your rights. This game is an exercise in releasing yourself from the imagined controls of others and taking charge of your actions.

Games for developing Wholeness

Wholeness is to be aware of your full potential. Behaving in a "holistic" way is to operate by using both "sides" of the brain - the thinking brain and the feeling brain. A whole person reasons in seriousness and senses playfully.

1

If viewed in a mirror, your reflection appears as a reverse image. But looking into a corner made by two mirrors at right angles will give you an exact image as others see you. Find or set up a corner mirror and study your true reflection while enjoying some SERIOUS PLAY. Go ahead, horse around. Try to detect and identify the serious you and the playful you.

2

Compare the two halves of your face for differences related to their opposing-controlling brain hemispheres. (Right-brain normally controls left side of body and vice-versa.)

3

Have a friend take two photographs of you. In one of them, pose as the intelligent, serious and self-controlled thinker you know yourself to be. In the second, respond to any urge for playfulness. Restraint is ruled out. Mount them side by side with appropriate titles and keep them within sight to remind you of your truly whole two-sided nature.

Games for Developing Freedom from Pride

PRIDE OFTEN LEADS US TO BEHAVE CONTRARY TO OUR FEELINGS. Try **to decide how you actually** feel about some matter of importance and allow that feeling to rule your behavior **in every situation** and contact. Don't behave one way in front of your friend, another in front of your employer, and still another in front of your mother. Stay loyal with your beliefs and express them consistently.

1 ASK A FRIEND TO VIDEO YOU involved in some ordinary activity like having a conversation on a telephone. Make sure that long shots, medium shots, and close-ups are included and that you can observe yourself from front, side, rear, below and above. This is one sure way to discover how different you actually are from what you may unrealistically imagine.

2 BREAK SOME FEAR HABITS:
A) DON'T ANSWER THE PHONE the next five times it rings. Instead, with each ring examine why the phone has such power over your attention.
B) SPEAK OUT. The next time someone says something that sounds or seems outrageous to you (something bigoted, insulting or fallacious), put it straight by speaking out. Simply state your objection as calmly as possible. A rehearsal might help forestall phony excuses or meanness brought on by anger.
C) PRIDE AND FEAR waste time. A boring lecture can become interesting if you join the act by asking questions.

Guide to Measurable

The CREATIVE PROBLEM-SOLVING process is best viewed as a series of activities (objectives) leading to a solution or goal. You begin with the tasks of Acceptance and Analysis and end with Ideation and Selection, Implementation and Evaluation. The central phase is Definition, your declaration of intent or desired outcome. Your goal doesn't tell you how to get there. It merely states where you want to end up...tomorrow, next month, five years from now, decades from now.

Objectives

GOALS, normally stated in non-measurable terms, are elusive. They tend to only be attained in stages, piece by piece, with each step treated as an OBJECTIVE. Making OBJECTIVES MEASURABLE is to translate them into specific activities. Think of objectives as the work necessary to reach a goal, i.e. when the objectives are clear and made measurable you can eventually reach a goal. For example, a college may define a degree (goal) as a curriculum of courses (objectives). In turn each course defines a separate objective necessary for receiving the degree.

EXERCISE:
List the objectives you might need to satisfy if you <u>intend to</u> reach each of the following goals:

Cooking a special meal for six friends.
Buying a motorcycle.
Learning to speak a foreign language.
Designing a vacation house.

Notice there are no specific directions in any of those ordinary goal statements. Each one must be translated into a step-by-step process of actions for getting there. To achieve the "special" meal or the "right" motorcycle you must further define both the <u>quantity and quality</u> of the actions required. Only in that way will you be able to <u>measure</u> the accomplishment of your overall goal. For instance, the first <u>objective</u> involved in achieving the "special meal" <u>goal</u> might be "to determine the likes and dislikes of the six friends, what they can and cannot eat, which of them are on a diet, etc." <u>When you have such a list, that single objective can be said to be met.</u> Then, on to the next objectives: the menu, buying the parts, cleaning house, etc., etc.

<u>OBJECTIVES outline the path to your goals.</u> But clear foresight is not always possible and anxiety over excessive work can easily take over. To lessen its impact and to better assess the amount of work remaining, stop occasionally to review your goals and the tasks already accomplished. Remember: It's always up to you to stay in charge of where you plan to go.

Some lessons learned from Problem-Solving...by experience

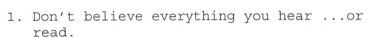

1. Don't believe everything you hear ...or read.

2. If you haven't been there before, you may have to feel your way slowly.

3. Having been there before can stop you from finding new ways to get there.

4. The solution of one problem might transfer to other kinds of problems.

5. Programmed process need not rule out "chance."

6. When Analysis leads to Definition, once impossible situations turn into solvable problems.

7. If you want insight, you have to break through the surfaces of things.

8. Obvious answers are often the hardest to find.

9. Different points of view are seen through different sets of eyes.

10. It is easy to look. To see takes effort. Creative thoughts come from seeing with 'fresh' eyes.

11. There are more ways than one to get to the same place.

12. Facts and understanding are closely connected.

13. One thing leads to another. Follow the clues.

14. Until translated into lessons, unpleasant memories can block discovery.

15. Intuition is the subconscious accumulation of past experiences. Great experiences lead to deeper feelings.

16. All experience is permanently locked in the brain waiting to be called into service.

by logic

1. A subconscious random sample of thoughts can stimulate a need for order.

2. It makes sense to set limits to every intention.

3. Thinking in itself does not evoke creativity which also depends on feeling

4. Trying to solve one thing is often accomplished by solving something else.

5. When you examine only part of a problem, it's a good idea to keep the whole problem in mind.

6. Proper assessment of all ideas is essential.

7. Losing your guide (security and habit) is one way to discover new paths.

8. A successful problem solution is dependent on the relationship of many sub-solutions.

9. There is always some form of relationship between all things.

10. The solution to one problem often opens the possibility for new problems to occur.

11. It is easier to reach a goal when the path of objectives is clear.

12. A weak understanding can lead to an ineffective conclusion.

13. Clear judgment requires clear standards.

14. The "playful you" is always there to help when the "logical you" gets stuck.

15. Solving the components can solve entire systems.

16. To determine the solution to a mystery, you must find the essential clues.

17. Some problems require side-trips into strange new territory before they can be resolved.

18. Finding simple ways to deal with complex situations is always possible.

19. Some problems are so connected to other problems that they cannot be considered by themselves alone.

20. A well-kept journal of a process provides an automatic product.

by planning

1. Principles and rules take many different forms.
2. Experiments can be costly but worth every cent.
3. Unrelated principles can block relevant principles.
4. Unpleasant journeys leave few good memories.
5. Perfect balance is theoretical. Reality is dynamic.
6. Complex problems can be simply defined.
7. A unique point of view is often found within existing points of view.
8. Some things just can't be dealt with properly when taken out of context.
9. Experience can sometimes lead to premature and incorrect conclusions.
10. Playing-around will at least get you moving.
11. To learn by doing you must first get started.
12. Clear thinking relies on balancing logic with experience.
13. Unproven principles can get you into trouble.
14. Expect the unexpected. Change is the only constant.
15. Know what you don't know. Dealing consciously with your ignorance develops awareness.
16. Perception and reality are never equal.
17. Good record-keeping prolongs the appreciation of experience.

SYNECTICS...

Among the many separate problem-solving processes synthesized into the "universal" process presented in this book, SYNECTICS, a means of formulating new views of problematic situations, looms as among the most important in terms of stimulating creative behavior.

Employing ANALOGY, METAPHOR, and SIMILE to develop unique solutions, alternatives and fresh viewpoints, Synectics is loosely translated as "the joining together of apparently different and irrelevant objects". Originated by William J.J. Gordon, the SYNECTICS process is described as an "excursion" through a sequence of three stages.

STAGE 1 — EXAMINE initial viewpoints.
Analyze the situation.
Criticize and unload preconceptions and restate the initial viewpoint.

STAGE 2 — "STRETCH" your limits by examining other problem situations without concern for your own situation. Get far away from the situation that is troubling you.

STAGE 3 — RETURN to the restated viewpoint with fresh experiences of other situations. Apply your understanding of other things to your own situation. Form a fresh viewpoint.

In short, SYNECTICS is a process of developing "insight" by utilizing the technique of "outsight." The key to this process is the to "stretch;" a psychological device based on the premise that it is easier to work on problems other than your own and then profit by applying those solutions derived outside of your situation to those within it.

According to Gordon, four paths to creative behavior are:

1. DETACHMENT AND INVOLVEMENT
Getting both outside the problem as well as inside the problem

2. DEFERMENT
Having tolerance for all manner of input

3. SPECULATION
Having fantasies; posing questions; making suppositions

4. OBJECT AUTONOMY
Allowing the product being sought to become the process being experienced

The three "MECHANISMS" for facilitation are:

1. DIRECT ANALOGY
Discovering how one thing is related to another develops awareness of the connection between all things.

2. PERSONAL ANALOGY
Role-playing, often to the point of empathy, develops an understanding of the situational conditions of a problem and helps reveal internal problems difficult to see from the outside.

3. COMPRESSED CONFLICT
Dealing with sub-problems can resolve the overall problem via eliminating internal conflict.

To utilize SYNECTICS techniques for generating fresh points-of-view regarding your problems, begin by asking how your situation is similar to a very different thing while remembering to "stretch" as far as you can. For example, a problem in human relations might find unique connections in the far corners of agriculture or mechanical engineering. Asking how a financial problem is like a plate of spaghetti is more likely to reveal a fresh viewpoint than if you tried to keep your attention glued to monetary matters.

Step outside your problem to get inside of it. Allow yourself to "feel" the uniqueness of related people, things, and situations.

Things always feel different when wearing someone else's shoes.

Procedure for Self-Hypnosis

Hypnosis is a universal device for reaching the subconscious with messages from the brain; it is the key to all forms of mental manipulation including all-important self-control. Prayer, meditation, EEG feedback, mind control, reevaluation counseling, Zen, karate, yoga, almost all positive thinking techniques, begin with hypnosis in one form or another. Hypnosis can't make you go against your own will. Rather, it helps you hear what your will is saying and overcome it if, or when, necessary. Essentially simple and painless, self-hypnosis merely requires focus; i.e., directing yourself to pay attention to changes in your behavior.

It's just a matter of getting yourself into a "receptive state" and when ready, telling you what to do and to begin imagining doing it. Memory of such 'virtual' experience later leads to actual experience in practice.

Freeing you from distraction and fear, as well as being a relaxation technique and primary self-improvement method, hypnosis can serve you at every stage of the creative problem-solving process.

PROCEDURE
(Approximate time: 20 minutes)

1. Begin by stating (perhaps in writing) your purpose. What is your intended "focus"?
2. Get into the hypnotic state of body and mind.

116

Lie down or lean back. Loosen up. Close your eyes. Allow reality to slip away. Relax progressively starting at the top of your head to the tips of your toes. Imagine counting slowly backwards from 100. Think of being on a slow-moving elevator descending floor by floor from the 100th Floor of an office building.

3. When nearly asleep, talk to yourself in a soft but firm tone, stating what it is that you wish to happen.

4. Virtually experience your wish via a mental scenario as though already realized. Enjoy the achievement.

5. Awaken with new or renewed confidence.

How to Criticize Painlessly

The need for assertiveness and self-protection is often at odds with other social needs and relations. Judgment and criticism, being major aspects of creative problem-solving, can unfortunately lead to hurt feelings and severed friendships if not offered in an acceptable form.

Here is a fool-proof method for telling yourself or someone else that something is wrong without fear of losing a friendship or starting a battle. It beats anger and intolerance hands down. The trick is to apply diplomacy and insert the criticism within a context of compliments.

1. BEGIN WITH TWO POSITIVE REINFORCEMENTS
"You really are a well-seasoned traveler."
"You have all of the best gear for hiking."

2. INSERT YOUR CRITICISM
"I wish we could stay in step when we hike together."

3. ADD ONE MORE POSITIVE REINFORCEMENT
"I notice that you adapt easily to most things."

4. FINISH WITH A RAY OF HOPE
"If we work on this together, I'm sure things will work out for the best."

Practice on a friend!

117

How to Accept Criticism

As the old saying goes, "it's easier to give criticism than to receive it." To verbally express discontent about something rather than to accept the challenge of constructively improving it physically is simply normal. It is also normal to be "defensive" of your position when criticized.

Instead of wasting time with defenses and the soothing of imaginary hurts, be creative and get procedural.

ACCEPT critical comments for further ANALYSIS and DEFINITION. If the criticism proves to be constructive, FIND A WAY to correct the problem and IMPLEMENT instead of rebelling against it. But, if found to be unwarranted or irrelevant, discard it and the matter is finished.

A Communications Checklist

Communication is tricky at best. Translating a meaning or message via a medium or media through an environment to an intended receiver is a process affected by many influences or factors.

The Basics

a

SENDER (Your knowledge and attitudes)
and
SENDER'S ABILITY to shape and convey the
message

b

RECEIVER (knowledge and attitudes)
and
RECEIVER'S ABILITY TO RECEIVE

c

MESSAGE QUALITY (substance and relevance)
Content: completeness
Relevance to receiver familiarity
Facilitates recognition
      clarity
      simplicity
      orderly
      strength of delivery

d

CHARACTERISTICS OF THE MEDIUM
Potential for sensory stimulation
Appropriateness to message content
Appropriateness to sender's skills, knowl-
edge and attitudes
Within ability of receiver to accept
Energy required
Symbolic characteristics
Speed
Noise (distraction) characteristics

e

THE ENVIRONMENT (external elements that
might facilitate or block the message)
Harmony with message and sender-receiver
relationship
Pressure to perform
Noise (distractions)
      movement
      sound interference
      temperature discomfort
      threat to physical or mental security

SOME OTHER FACTORS AFFECTING COMMUNICATION

Tone of voice
Age or age difference between sender and receiver
Personal relationship between sender and receiver
Expectation of either side based on experience
Choice and use of language: stance, slang, expletives
Apparent consequences of message
Hidden Agenda: motives, values, needs
Mood: recent uplifts, traumas, sickness, diversions,   fatigue, anxiety, etc.
Habits, customs, rituals, taboos, prejudices, biases, assumptions
Personal dress and grooming

Education, travel experience, breadth of outlook
Influential aspects: idols, models, aspirations
National, religious, ethnic, or racial heritage
Social attitudes, politics
Personal insecurities and/or strengths
Specific knowledge of message area
Mutual focus of attention

Need PEP ?? try...

...perhaps you need help with DIET planning or PHYSICAL FITNESS and need to consult a nutritionist, physical therapist or physician involved with preventive medicine

...maybe you have a HANG-UP or mental barrier and should visit a psychologist, psychiatrist, counseling center, religious advisor, or simply dial a local HOTLINE for assistance.

...you might need other SPECIALIZED help from local police, city administrators, consumer protection agency, men's, women's, or minority organizations, librarian, credit union, bank manager, a toll-free (800) telephone call to another part of the country, Internet search. Etc.

Wiring Diagrams

Some things never change. The human search for direction, pattern and order is a constant task. In the process, your experience translates into guidelines called "rules of thumb" which then serve as basic frames of reference when coping with new experience. They provide a creative head start when attempting to derive meaning from the bits and pieces of day-to-day problem-solving. It's often referred to as 'being wired."

WIRING DIAGRAMS simplify life. R. Buckminster Fuller reminds us that the only true specialist is the generalist. He suggests beginning with a good engineering handbook of basic physical and mathematical rules and relationships. We suggest that you start by recording those rules you already use and continue filling your personal bag of generalized principles as regularly as possible.

One commonly used and familiar example of a WIRING DIAGRAM is to know the path of the sun; that it rises in the east and sets in the west. When the sun or a shadow is visible such knowledge becomes a valuable substitute for compass, calendar, clock as well as a guide for planning adaptations to problems of weather and comfort.

THREE LEVELS OF HUMAN AWARENESS:

ATTRACTION
Become
Develop

UNDERSTANDING
Attracted
Meaning

MANIPULATION
Apply
discovery

●

FOUR WAYS OF VIEWING THE FUTURE:

1. Things will go on as they are...but will increase in size and benefits.
2. Same as 1, but things will get worse instead of better.
3. Some marvelous inventions will turn your life into a wondrous new existence.
4. The future is the result of your plans and efforts.

●

COMPOSITION:

Human response to patterns observed in Nature;

HARMONY
...a recognizable similarity among the parts of a whole...there needs to be a consistency of language or idiom in any synthesis intended to communicate harmony

CONTRAST
...a recognizable difference among the parts of a whole...the need for active conflict or difference to stimulate attention

BALANCE
... a recognizable equilibrium...the need for stability of interrelationships

ORDER
...a recognizable pattern of organization...the need for systematic operations

UNITY
...a recognizable wholeness or "oneness"; the need to suggest completeness or totality

●

THREE ASPECTS OF HUMAN EXPERIENCE:

SKILLS, KNOWLEDGE, AND ATTITUDE
What you can do, what you know, and what you believe

BASIC HUMAN NEEDS

Creative Problem-solvers never lose sight of basic human needs. (Abraham Maslow, Jean Piaget, et al) Having an improved alarm clock has little meaning to someone kept awake by hunger. In a normal hierarchy of need, they are: FOOD, THIRST, SLEEP, SHELTER, SECURITY, BELONGING, LOVE, ESTEEM, STATUS, and SELF-ACTUALIZATION

●

GESTALT RULES OF VISUAL ORGANIZATLON

Clear visual perception requires:
SIMILARITY
Something alike about the parts of the whole
PROXIMITY
Close togetherness rather than wide apartness of the components of the thing being organized
CLOSED FORMS
All parts seen as complete and not partial, singular parts becoming wholes
GOOD CONTOURS
Enclosures and lines must not be so complex or amorphous as to be difficult to reform in the mind
COMMON MOVEMENTS
All parts should operate within the same organizational patterns
RELEVANT EXPERIENCE
We tend to see only that which we are programmed to see

●

THREE STEPS TO SELF-CONTROL AND PERSONAL CHANGE:

RELAXATION: giving yourself over to the process; not holding back; making friends with the situation (Acceptance)
IMAGINATION: using **your** ability to form images that vividly describe the changes you desire; having intentional pictures of your dreams (Analysis)
CONCENTRATION: bringing your attention and energy to focus on your intentions (Synthesis)

Wiring Ahead

Use these pages to begin your personal collection of 'wiring diagrams', especially those you believe have potential for simplifying future creative problem-solving journeys.

Wiring Back

If you have learned to be more organized
and creative while reading these pages, you
should be anxious to do something "constructive" about one or more of your "dis-
contents." If you'd like to tell us how to
improve some part of this book, we'd like
to hear your thoughts. The 'method' that
works best is "Write it down and mail it to
us". By writing your discontent you will
also give yourself the opportunity to see
whether or not your words are as good—or as
bad—as your feelings. We'll respond, if at
all possible, to your feedback.

Send feedback to...

The Universal Travelers
C/o Crisp Publications, Inc.
1200 Hamilton Court
Menlo Park, CA 94025

Or

Don Koberg or Jim Bagnall,
Professors Emeriti
California Polytechnic State University
College of Architecture
and Environmental Design
San Luis Obispo, CA 93407

127

128